THE MAKING OF NEW ENGLAND

1580-1643

CUTTYHUNK ISLAND - SITE OF THE FIRST NEW ENGLAND COLONY.

THE

MAKING OF NEW ENGLAND

1580–1643

BY

SAMUEL ADAMS DRAKE

WITH MANY ILLUSTRATIONS AND MAPS

NEW YORK

CHARLES SCRIBNER'S SONS

1896

Presswork by Berwick & Smith,
Boston, U.S.A.

THE MAKING OF NEW ENGLAND

By Samuel Adams Drake

As Published in 1896

Trade Paperback ISBN: 1-58218-398-8
Hardcover ISBN: 1-58218-399-6
eBook ISBN: 1-58218-397-X

Digital Scanning and Publishing is a leader in the electronic republication of historical books and documents. We publish many of our titles as eBooks, as well as traditional hardcover and trade paper editions. DSI is committed to bringing many traditional and little known books back to life, retaining the look and feel of the original work.

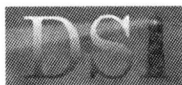

©2001 DSI Digital Reproduction
First DSI Printing: June 2001

Published by DIGITAL SCANNING, INC.
Scituate, MA 02066
Toll free: 888-349-4443
Outside U.S. 781-545-2100
www.digitalscanning.com

PREFACE.

"TELL THE TRUTH."

T HIS little book is intended to meet, so far as it may, the want of brief, compact, and handy manuals of the beginnings of our country.

It aims to occupy a place between the larger and the lesser histories,—to so condense, or eliminate from, the exhaustive narrative as to give it greater vitality, or so extend and elucidate what the school history too often leaves obscure for want of space as to supply the deficiency. So when teachers have a particular topic before them it is intended that a chapter on the same subject be read to fill out the bare outlines of the common-school text-book.

To this end the plan has been to treat each particular topic as a unit to be worked out to a clear understanding of its objects and results, before passing on to another topic. And in furtherance of this method each unit has its own descriptive notes, maps, plans, and pictorial illustration, of all of which liberal use is made, so that all may contribute to a thorough knowledge of the matter in hand.

The several topics readily fall into groups that have either an apparent or underlying historic connection, which is clearly brought out.

It has been well said that antiquity cannot privilege an error or novelty prejudice a truth. As it has seemed certainly better for our purpose to build with known and reliable materials than to encumber the story with loose conjectures or disputed traditions, introduced for the sake of picturesque effect, only such of the early attempts as had definite bearing upon colonization have been thought valuable aids to instruction.

Again, so much has been done in the past ten years to clear up what was before unsettled, that the time seems none too soon for going over the ground with the added light of recent and more thorough investigation.

Our narrative fully covers the critical periods of discovery, exploration, and settlement of New England from the earliest beginnings to the time when stable government, the security achieved by arms, and the development and adaptation of social or material ideas to the varied conditions of the new home had won for the first colonists a secure foothold in the New World.

A faithful record of what was done by the forefathers is not only full of interest to persons of mature age, but embodies the best lessons for the young. They see just how their country grew to be the great and prosperous nation it is to-day. The story is like that of a child learning to walk. At first feeble and tottering, the stripling at length grows bold and vigorous and his step assured as that of manhood. But the child was father to the man. The little seed which the Pilgrim Fathers planted in misgiving and nursed in fear has increased and borne fruit on the shores of the Pacific, and the parent tree still puts forth its blossoms no less vigorously than of old.

To enhance the interest of this story, emphasis has been given to every thing that went to make up the home life of the pioneer settlers or relates to their various avocations. To know how these men lived is to know the secret process by which the New England character was so moulded as to eventually become a national force as well as type.

MORIONS OF THE DISCOVERY PERIOD.

CONTENTS.

CONTENTS.

LIST OF ILLUSTRATIONS.

ix

ANCIENT SYMBOL OF NEW ENGLAND.

I.

WESTWARD HO!

THE MYSTIC COAST OF CODFISH.

"Westward the course of empire takes its way."

IT is no very uncommon thing for a man to live to be a hundred years old. If we consider that the united lives of three such men would more than span the whole period of time since the first attempt was made to plant a colony in New England, we shall bring home to ourselves, sharply and clearly, the fact that the history of New England, as compared with that of Old England, is quite recent history.

There is, however, a history going back to a very remote time,—how remote no one can say. But that is lost. All we know is that the country itself was peopled, when our forefathers first came to it,

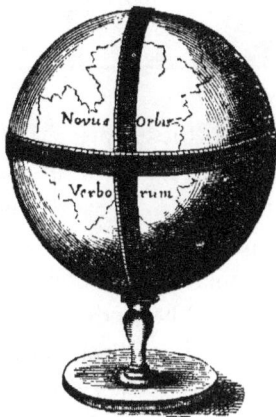

by a race differing from our own in color, in language, in manners, in religion, and in almost every thing by which one people is distinguished from another people. They could neither read nor write. They had no way of preserving an account of what had happened to them in the past but by word of mouth, or tradition. The old men told the story to the young men, who in turn repeated it to their children, and so it has come down from generation to generation, until these traditions have at last been written down, not by the Indians, but by the whites who came to occupy their country. So all we actually know of this singular people is what the whites learned after their arrival among them. Farther back than this we cannot go.

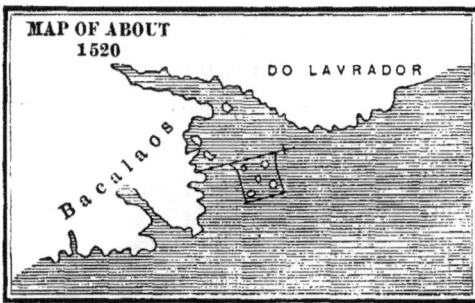

MAP OF ABOUT 1520

DO LAVRADOR

Bacalaos

COAST OF CODFISH.

Our ancestors called these primitive people "savages," because they lived almost in a state of nature. They called them "heathens," because they were ignorant of the Christian religion. They called them "Indians," because this continent was supposed by the first discoverers to be a part of the Indies.[1]

The English claimed the country as theirs, by reason of its discovery in the reign of Henry VII.,[2] just the same as if it had been uninhabited or unpossessed by any other people. And their doing so was in accord with the custom of all civilized nations at that time. It was a custom based upon might, not right, but growing out of the idea that it was the duty of all Christian peoples to subdue and civilize the barbarous races. Therefore from the moment of its discovery the new country was opened to all English subjects who should wish to go there, upon such conditions as the King might choose to make.

Yet on the first day of the new year 1602 not a single English settlement existed in all the wide continent which England had added to her dominions more than a century before.

It was the stories carried home by the earliest navigators, that the seas of these unknown coasts were swarming with codfish, that sent the intrepid mariners of Europe hither. They were simply fishermen. Across the wide and stormy ocean, in little vessels of only twenty and thirty tons burden, they took their adventurous way to the Coast of Codfish, or Baccalos, as the Breton and Norman sailors then called it. Beginning with Labrador and Newfoundland, these toilers of the sea slowly felt their way along the shores with line and lead as far as Massachusetts Bay, coming with the

BRETON FISHERMAN.

spring, flitting with the autumn, but carrying home the cargoes that gave evidence of wealth greater than the mines of Mexico or Peru. Such was the beginning.

Shakspeare mentions the codfish by the name of "Poor John." Cervantes makes his knight-errant Don Quixote partake of a dinner of the kind called in Andalusia baccalaos, because the day was Friday, on which no good Catholic would eat meat.

How did these pathfinders of the sea designate New England? Had this unknown region a name? Yes. Long before any Englishman is known to have set foot

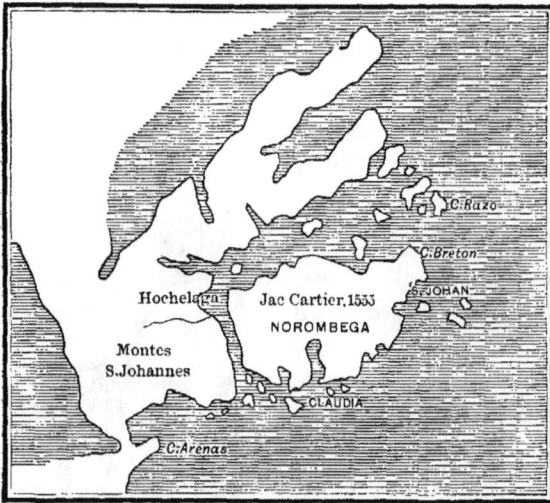

NOROMBEGA, 1582

upon it, the barbarous name of Norombega is laid down upon very ancient maps. Whence or how it came there is a mystery. But there it is on map after map, with one great river flowing out of it to the sea. It was described by the old geographers as a very fertile and populous region, surrounded with shallow and dangerous seas, so full of fish that boats could not have free passage among them.

But it is hardly worth while to dwell upon this ancient and obscure name, because it disappeared from the maps as soon as accurate knowledge of the country was obtained. If it had any meaning at all, it was lost with those who gave it. So that, much as we should like to know its origin, this name of Norombega is rather curious than instructive. Still, it is the earliest name by which New England was known, and as such will keep its place and history.

As for the work of the map-makers of the sixteenth century, so far as it relates to New England nothing like its true outline is anywhere given. But these maps do show us that our coasts were visited by Christian mariners at a very early day.

[1] Indies. Columbus supposed he had discovered some part of Asia, which was the object of his voyage. Hence he called the islands he found West Indies, and the native race Indians.

[2] Cabot's voyage of 1497. Like Columbus, he was trying to get to India. It is not known what land he discovered, though C. Breton is designated on a map of Sebastian Cabot (1514).

THE LAND CALLED NORTH VIRGINIA.

W ITH the daring spirits of Elizabeth's reign,—the Drakes, the Frobishers, the Hawkinses,—the movement to colonize the new found land had its inglorious beginning. Their buccaneering exploits, and the rich booty brought home from the plunder of galleons, cathedrals, or castles, had revived the piratical spirit of the old Norse sea-rovers throughout all England. Hope of gain sent adventurers into distant seas, and eager colonists to search out new lands. As Shakspeare then wrote,—

"Some to the wars, to try their fortune there;
Some to discover islands far away."

Toward the end of Elizabeth's reign two very remarkable men, Sir Humphrey Gilbert and Sir Walter Raleigh, determined to attempt an English settlement in North America. Queen Bess, as her subjects loved to call her, gave Gilbert leave to go and take possession of Newfoundland in her name. Gilbert did so, but he afterward perished in a storm at sea, calmly reading his Bible as the ship went down.[1]

> "'Do not fear! Heaven is as near,'
> He said, 'by water as by land!'"

The Queen then gave Raleigh[2] a chance to make the trial, granting him a royal authority or patent[3] for the purpose. This patent gave Raleigh the exclusive right to plant colonies, or open a trade with those distant lands. His expedition landed on the South Coast. In the Queen's honor, and because she was a maiden sovereign, the whole territory lying between Florida and Nova Scotia was then called Virginia. After making great exertions, Raleigh failed to establish a permanent settlement. His failure, it is believed, led others who had the same object at heart with him to have faith that they could succeed in a different quarter. Said they: "Newfoundland is too cold, Virginia too hot, for Englishmen to live in. One is fit only for fishing, the other for raising tobacco. Why not find some place

SIR HUMPHREY GILBERT.

between, where the climate is more like that of England? Then we shall have no trouble in getting our countrymen to stay in it."

At last this idea took root in the minds of certain noblemen and captains who had knowledge of Raleigh's efforts. They resolved to direct their attempt to the north part of Virginia instead of the south. Virginia, then,

THE FIRST SHIP.

was the name by which New England first became known to Englishmen.

[1] Sir Humphrey Gilbert went to Newfoundland in 1583. See Longfellow's poem on Gilbert's shipwreck, while returning to England. His ship is supposed to have foundered at Sable Island, N.S.

[2] Sir Walter Raleigh never came to Virginia, though he made great efforts, and spent a great deal of money in trying to colonize it. He was beheaded by order of James I., 1618, for alleged treason and conspiracy.

[3] Patent, or Letters-Patent,—a grant from the sovereign of exclusive rights or powers to an individual, or body of individuals, to secure certain ends: in this case, to plant colonies. The original patent of Massachusetts may be seen in the Secretary of State's office at Boston.

GOSNOLD'S COLONY OF 1602.

"Quoth he there was a ship."

IT was on Friday, the 25th of March, 1602, then thought by mariners to be an unlucky day, that Captain Bartholomew Gosnold's ship unfurled her sails for North Virginia.

Fitted out as some say under favor of the noble Raleigh himself, Gosnold's parting words to his patron may well have been:

SETTING SAIL.

"My lord, I will hoiste saile; and all the wind
My bark can beare shall hasten me to find
A great New World!"

And very possibly as the little Concord glided from her moorings at Falmouth, in Cornwall, the cheery cry of her west-country boatswain was as Shakspeare gives it in the "Tempest":

"Heigh my hearts; cheerly, cheerly my hearts:
Yare, yare: tend to the master's whistle—
Blow till thou burst thy wind if room enough!"

Gosnold's whole company mustered only thirty-two men, all told, some of whom had sailed with Sir Francis Drake. Some twenty odd were colonists who had agreed to stay in the country they were going to settle in. Had Gosnold a definite destination? Undoubtedly he had.

It seems that in reading a narrative of Verrazano's voyage[1] to the New World Gosnold had been much struck with the praises of a certain port into which the friendly natives had piloted Verrazano's ship. Its fine anchorage, the fertility of its shores, and the friendly welcome he had met with, were all set forth at much length, for the fifteen days spent in refitting his ship had given Verrazano ample time to make explorations. He gives the latitude of this place as in 412/3°. We have every reason to think that Gosnold was going in search of this wonderful haven.

On the 14th of April Gosnold sighted the Azores.[2] Instead of following the old track, by way of the West Indies, he had the courage to steer due west by the compass from these islands. And this course would bring him to the place he wished to find.

JUAN VERRAZANO.

Day after day, league after league the good ship sailed on, with no sail but hers on all that wilderness of waters. The sailors saw nothing but sky and sea above and about them.

Great wonder was shown by Gosnold's men when one day they found the ship ploughing through vast fields of seaweed, which hurried past as if borne along by some mysterious current. This wonderful current, or river in the ocean, was the Gulf Stream, but Gosnold's sailors did not know of it and were amazed at the phenomenon.

On the 10th of May they struck soundings. From this time they sailed cautiously, often heaving the lead and keeping a lookout at the masthead during the day. At night they shortened sail, just keeping steerage way on the ship, for fear of grounding on some unknown shoal.

So they sailed with caution, having no chart to guide or landmark to lead them, until the 13th, when the quantity of drift stuff that floated by the ship and the delicious odor wafted over the sea convinced the sailors that they would see the shore on that day or the next.

So, indeed, it proved, for at six in the morning they saw the long, dark, line of coast stretching out before them as far as the eye could reach. They had crossed the ocean and reached the unknown shore in just forty-nine days.[3]

This day also was Friday. So they had not only sailed on Friday but, had their first sight of land on Friday.

As the Concord drew nearer, what was Gosnold's surprise to see a European shallop,[4] with mast and sail, coming off to the ship. His surprise was still greater when he saw that this boat, made by Christian hands, was manned only by naked savages. When they had come quite near, these strange beings hailed the ship, as sailors do. Captain Gosnold answered the hail. Then his men beckoned to the Indians to come on board, which they presently did without fear.

One only had on any clothing; and, strange to say, he was dressed like a European. All the rest were naked, except that each had a sealskin tied round his loins like a blacksmith's apron. All were tall, big-boned, active-looking men. They had reddish, or tan-colored skins, long, glossy, black hair, tied behind in a knot, and good, regular features, but no beards. Indeed, they would have been called fine-looking men, but for the strange custom of daubing their faces and bodies with paint, and afterwards smearing them with oil, which made them look less like men than demons.

One would have white eyebrows, vermilion lips and cheeks, a jet black nose, and possibly a blue, or parti-colored, forehead and chin. This custom meant nearly the same thing to the Indian that his armorial bearings did to the white man, but it went further than this because one Indian could tell whether another meant war or peace by the way he was painted.

None of these natives could speak English,

FISHING SHALLOP OF THE TIME.

but they could pronounce the word Placentia, which made Gosnold think that some French vessel from Placentia in Newfoundland [5] had been here already. Moreover, the shallop was a Basque,[6] or Biscay-built, boat, and the Indians knew how to handle it with the dexterity of old sailors.

These Indians had no weapons except bows and arrows—bows of stout ash, arrows headed with sharp flints.

Having neither pilot nor chart the captain made signs that he would like to know something about the lay of

the land. The Indians understood him. With a piece
of chalk one of them drew a rude chart of the coast on
the deck. After this, with many friendly nods, grins
and signs the savages went off in their shallop.

Finding himself far north of where he purposed going
Gosnold stood off to the southward during the rest of
the day and night. At day-
light the next morning the
ship was completely land
locked "within a mighty
headland" which Gosnold
at first thought must be an
island. He resolved to learn
if such was the fact. If this
land were an island there
must be an opening some-
where to the westward
through which he might sail.

SHIP AT ANCHOR.

So having anchored, he took the shallop, and with
John Brereton and three others, all well-armed, started
to explore this land which blocked his way. So far as
known these were the first Englishmen who had ever
trod the soil of New England.

The explorers had a weary tramp in their heavy armor,
but on climbing some of the nearest hills they saw that
what they had taken for an island was really a cape
with a broad bay on one side and the open sea on the
other. They then went back to the ship with their
news.

When they got on board again they found the deck
thick with codfish that the crew had been taking while
the explorers were gone. Seeing the great abundance
of these fish Gosnold gave the headland the name of

Cape Cod. In doing this he had conferred the very first English name given to any part of New England.

After this the Concord doubled the cape, though not without danger, for at one time she was near being lost among the shoals of Monomoy, which were long a terror to all navigators of this coast.

Escaping from these perils, the discoverers continued to feel their way along the shore, now and then receiving visits from the natives in their canoes,[7] or seeing them run along the shore in their eagerness to keep the strange ship in sight. Presently they entered the narrow sea which on account of Gosnold's visit has taken the name of the Vineyard Sound.

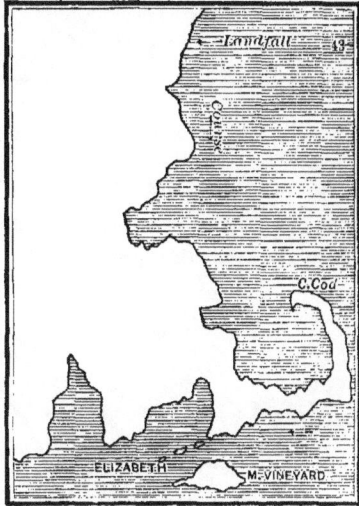

WHAT GOSNOLD DID.

With eager eyes the colonists looked upon the lovely scene before them, for here at last was their home beyond the sea. The first great island they came to was christened Martha's Vineyard.[8]

[For geographical names outside of New England, consult the atlas or Lippincott's Gazetteer.]

[1] VERRAZANO'S VOYAGE was made by order of Francis I. of France. He fell in with the coast near Cape May and ascended it as far as Nova Scotia. His ship probably anchored in the harbor of Newport, R.I.

[2] AZORES, islands in the North Atlantic belonging to Portugal, sometimes called Western Islands. A celebrated stopping-place for the early navigators in going to America.

[3] GOSNOLD'S LANDFALL was probably not far north of Cape Ann.

[4] SHALLOP, a boat with sail, mast, and oars, but no deck, and used for fishing

and coasting. Some carried twenty or more men.

5 NEWFOUNDLAND was frequented by the French and Portuguese long before Sir H. Gilbert took possession.

6 BASQUES, a people inhabiting the French and Spanish provinces of the Bay of Biscay, and having a curious language of their own.

7 CANOE, a light boat, sometimes made of birch-bark, stretched upon a wooden frame, sometimes of a log hollowed out with fire.

8 MARTHA'S VINEYARD. It is not known whom Gosnold meant to honor by this name. The relations of his companionsafford no clew, nor does Gosnold himself throw any light upon the subject.

GOSNOLD'S COLONY—*Continued.*

As soon as the sails had been furled Captain Gosnold went on shore to look for a place that would best meet the wants of the settlers. Every thing was in a state of

MAKING A WIGWAM.—INDIAN CRADLE.

savage wildness, but every thing announced a goodly land to dwell in.

There were great oaks and stately pines, luxuriant shrubbery and climbing vines, strawberries "bigger than in England," raspberries, gooseberries and huckleberries, all growing in wild profusion. Deer bounded through the thickets. Water-fowl were never seen in such numbers before.

Gosnold saw only one solitary hut made of bent saplings covered with bark. Near this wigwam[1] he found an abandoned fish-weir[2] and he also saw where fires had been kindled.

The chain of islands lying next the mainland was then explored. Of fish, flesh, fowl, and fruits, there promised to be no want. Beautiful flowers blossomed on unknown plants which on being pulled up showed the finders forty or more ground-nuts growing on a sin-

CUTTYHUNK, GOSNOLD'S ISLAND

gle root. Mussels, lobsters, clams, oysters, and scollops were to be had for the trouble of gathering them. Firewood and pure water were also plentiful.

By reason of its greater security, should the savages prove unfriendly, Gosnold made choice of one of the smaller islands for a residence. In honor of Queen Bess he called it Elizabeth,[3] but this name has since been transferred to the whole group. At one end of this island there was a fresh water pond, and in this pond a little rocky islet. In this sequestered nook, where they would be doubly secure, the colonists began to build their storehouse and erect their fort.

While Brereton with ten men was doing this, Gosnold ranged through the islands searching for sassafras,[4] which was then worth a great price in England. It was soon found by one of his men, who hastened to report his discovery to the captain.

SASSAFRAS PLANT.

On one of his excursions Gosnold went over to the mainland, where he met some Indians, whose good will he gained with gifts. So eager were they to possess a knife that they willingly gave a beaver-skin[5] in exchange. In this way, a trade sprung up between them and the whites.

During this trip Gosnold found that the islands enclosed a large body of water[6] which extended far into the land. But he did not have time to explore it.

A few days after landing, fifty Indians visited the colonists on the island. They came in eleven canoes. Not wishing them to see their fort, the colonists went to meet them. When the Indians came on shore they all squatted on their heels like a pack of expectant hounds. The English brought them meat and tried to enter-

CANOE.

tain them royally. They ate heartily of every thing, but the mustard nipped their noses so sharply and caused them to make such wry faces that it was laughable to see them.

After eating, the savages lit their pipes and smoked with much content. They gave some of their tobacco [7] to the whites, who found it very pleasant indeed. When it grew dark the Indians went to the opposite end of the island, where they kindled fires by striking two stones together until the sparks lit a piece of touch-wood, or tinder, which was nearly the same method practised by Europeans with steel and tinder. Each savage took with him in a little bag his stones and punk. They roasted crabs and groundnuts, and broiled herrings on the coals, which they ate with great relish. They drank out of cups that looked like skulls, but were probably only skull-shaped gourds. When they had finished their meal they grouped themselves about the fires, and stretched their naked bodies upon the bare ground, as free from care as the other inhabitants of the island. And this was the way these simple sons of the forest lived in summer, roaming like Nomads from place to place, but oftener spending the whole season in some favorite spot, where the huge shell-heaps show to this day what was their manner of life.

The white men of course took note of every thing about the Indians, while the Indians with equal curi-osity watched every action of the whites. The whites were much surprised to find some of the savages wear-ing copper armor, or ornaments, very curiously wrought. They thought there must be mines of copper some-where about, and this added to the interest of their discovery. One Indian wore a copper breastplate; others had chains or collars made of many hollow pieces joined together somewhat after the manner of a soldier's bandoleer. [8]   Still others had ear-rings and arrow-heads of copper. So the Indians clearly had one metal which they had learned to use, and possibly they knew of the more precious metals which the whites were so anxious to obtain.

Being armed with muskets, swords, pikes and targets, the English did not fear the more numerous savages, and in a fair fight would have come off victors. But they did fear treachery and so kept a sharp lookout.

On the fourth day the Indians left the island. They pointed five times to the sun and then over to the mainland, which was their way of saying that they would come back in five days. After paddling off a short distance they all gave a great shout, to which Gosnold's men replied by a blast from their trumpets and shooting off their pieces and tossing their caps in the air.

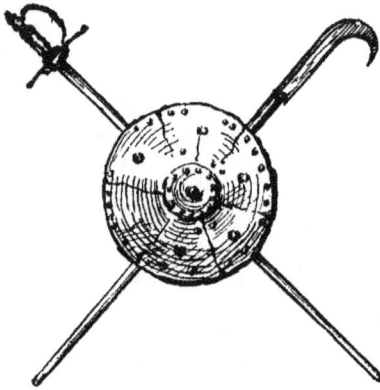

TARGET, SWORD, AND WOLF-HOOK.

So far all had gone prosperously. The men were in good health and spirits. With the furs and skins obtained by barter, enough sassafras and cedarwood had been put aboard the ship to make a good showing for the voyage, and they were impatient to meet their friends in England, and report the news. In nineteen days their storehouse had been completed and they were ready to sail.

But by this time some who had agreed to stay in the country had changed their minds, and now wished to return in the ship. Some had been shot at by the Indians, and began to feel they might be cut off or in some way destroyed. Some pretended that there was a plot to abandon them, and expressed fear that the ship would never return. Some made one excuse and some another. Upon a survey of the stores it was found that not enough would be left to feed the colonists until the ship could go to England and return, and as only twelve men were willing to stay with him, Gosnold reluctantly gave order to abandon the settlement, which accordingly was done, and on Friday the 18th of June the whole company turned from the shores they had come to with glowing hopes of a prosperous settlement.

---

[1] WIGWAM, an Indian house made of poles planted in the ground in a circle. By bringing the ends together at the top, the frame was ready for the covering, which was sometimes bark, sometimes coarse rush mats.

[2] FISH-WEIR, made by planting poles or boughs in the bed of a tidal stream, so close together as to stop the fish at the fall of the tide. A sort of fish pound.

[3] ELIZABETH ISLANDS, now the town of Gosnold. They have Indian names:
Cuttyhunk and Penakese,
Nashawena, Pasquenese,
Great Naushon, Nonamesset,
Uncatena and Wepecket.

[4] SASSAFRAS was highly valued for its medicinal properties and then worth three shillings the pound in England.

[5] BEAVER-SKIN. The beaver was then much the most valuable fur-bearing animal in the country, and its skin was highly prized in Europe. It therefore became the chief article of commerce between Indians and whites. At first numerous, the animal grew scarce and finally became extinct through the indiscriminate slaughter made of both sexes. The Indians held it in veneration on account of its superior intelligence, which in some respects was almost human.

[6] BUZZARD'S BAY is meant.

[7] TOBACCO. The New-England Indians did not cultivate the Virginia plant, but smoked a wild sort, called Poke. Their pipes were made of red and white clay, baked in the sun.

[8] BANDOLEER, a belt containing little pouches, each holding a charge of powder. Very similar belts are now worn by sportsmen to carry cartridges.

THE FIRST WINTER.—DE MONTS' COLONY, 1604.

W E will now follow the fortunes of a noble French gentleman, the Sieur De Monts,[1] in his attempt to plant a colony in a remote corner of New England.

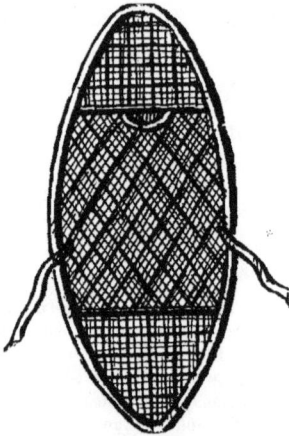

It must be kept in mind that the French did not acknowledge the right of England to what was then called North Virginia, but held that Verrazano had discovered it the first and that it belonged to them. And on their maps it was actually called New France.[2]

Emulating the example of the Spaniards in Florida, and the English in Virginia, the French had been pushing their way into Canada for many years, by way of the great river St. Lawrence, with very indifferent success. Its winter climate was so cold, its navigable waters were so early and so long frozen up, that some of the more sagacious ones thought that a settlement farther south would have a much better chance. The Chevalier De Monts was of this opinion, and he made known his views to the king.[3]

We should also remember that while the general name then given to the French possessions in Canada was New France, that particular part to which De Monts intended going was now called La Cadie, or Acadie.

King Henry IV. granted De Monts a patent, under

INDIAN SNOW-SHOE.

the broad seal, which covered all the country now included in New England, and much besides. In order that he might carry out his plans, his majesty, the king, also granted De Monts a monopoly of the fur trade in those parts.

With this grant in his possession, De Monts secured the aid of certain merchants who furnished him with the means, in whole or in part, for equipping two vessels with every thing needful for his colony. Nothing that experience or foresight could counsel was omitted to make this colony a success.

Having collected above a hundred followers, good and bad,[4] of whom some were artisans, some laborers, some sol-

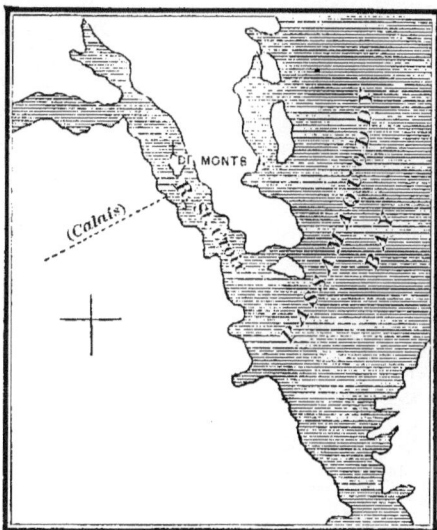

WHERE DE MONTS SETTLED.

diers and others gentlemen going for love of adventure, De Monts embarked them at Havre de Grace with order to the masters to meet at Canso in Cape Breton. They set sail in the month of April 1604, and arrived at the rendezvous early in May.

As one of De Monts' companions makes a bright figure in history, we will now mention him briefly. This gentleman was Samuel de Champlain.[5] Of all the early explorers, New England is most indebted to him. And though he sought to advance only the glory of France, his memory belongs to us no less than to his own countrymen; for what he did has at length become an inseparable part of our own history.

So we see men of a rival nation coming to lay hold on the soil of New England.

Soon after their arrival, Champlain was sent to search the coasts farther west in a little bark fitted out for the purpose. De Monts presently joined him. Together they examined the Bay of Fundy, went into the Annapolis Basin, into the St. John and afterwards Passamaquoddy Bay,[6] up which they sailed into the mouth of another fine river.

On their way hither they passed by so many islands that they were not able to count them. Sailing on a league or two up this river they came to a small island lying in the middle of it.

POWDER FLASK

Pleased with its situation, charmed with the prospect around them, they resolved to make their home here, upon this spot. De Monts then and there gave the island the name of St. Croix.[7]

Sending back for his vessel and his colonists to come to him, De Monts immediately began building a barricade across the island with those he had then with him.

Champlain was appointed to lay out the ground. As soon as the others had joined him the work of building a storehouse, dwellings and fort was begun in earnest. All worked so energetically that the place was speedily put in a condition for defence, though the men were much pestered by mosquitoes, whose bites caused their faces to swell so that they could hardly see out of their eyes.

While the forests around were echoing to the vigorous strokes of the axe and the hammer and every thing denoted bustle on the island, Champlain was again sent to make further exploration of the coast beyond. He took twelve sailors and two savages of the country to act as interpreters. After sailing on through a multitude of islands he came at last to a very large and commanding one which rose from the sea into a cluster of naked mountain peaks. He quickly saw that it was one of the natural landmarks of the coast, and he therefore gave it the name which it still bears of Monts Déserts. [8]

Here the Frenchmen met with Indians who were shy at first, but whose fears they soon quieted with gifts. These Indians guided Champlain into their river, called by them Pentegouet. [9]   And what a noble stream it was! Its deep tide flowed on to the sea as it had done amid the silence of ages. On all sides pleasant isles and fine meadows, tall forests and lofty mountains, charmed the eyes of the explorers. Yet neither town nor villages nor scarcely any sign of a human habitation was to be seen. All was as wild as at the Creation.

Champlain sailed many leagues up this brave river until he came to a waterfall which obstructed its navigation. [10]   From the accounts he had read of it in the old chronicles, he had expected to find a large and populous city situated somewhere in this river, but instead of a city he saw only here and there a wretched cabin and now and then only a solitary Indian. Yet this was probably the locality assigned by the geographers of Champlain's time, and long before him, to the fabulous city of Norombega,[11] which they asserted to be so great and populous as to have given its name to the whole surrounding region.

The savages who had conducted Champlain to the falls now went away in order to notify their chief of his arrival. Soon this chief came with many others in his train to see who these strange white men were and what they wanted. De Monts and Champlain knew that to live in the country they must conciliate the natives. So Champlain talked with them as well as he could. He told them that the French had come to dwell with them in their land, and would show the Indians how to cultivate it so as to live less miserably than they were doing. The Indians seemed well pleased with all Champlain said to them, but they were delighted when he gave them a few knives, hatchets, caps and knick-knacks in token of good will—so much so that they did nothing but dance and sing all the rest of the day and night.

Learning that there was another great river, still farther west, which the natives called Quin′i′be′qui, Champlain set sail for it, but after going a few leagues bad weather forced him to turn back without reaching it. In the mean time he saw and named Isle au Haut.[12]

It was now October. Meanwhile the settlers had completed their houses. They had left an oblong open plot of ground in the middle of the settlement. In the

centre of this stood a large tree. On one side were
the dwelling of De Monts, the storehouse and the ba-
kery, on the other side the curate's dwelling, the well,

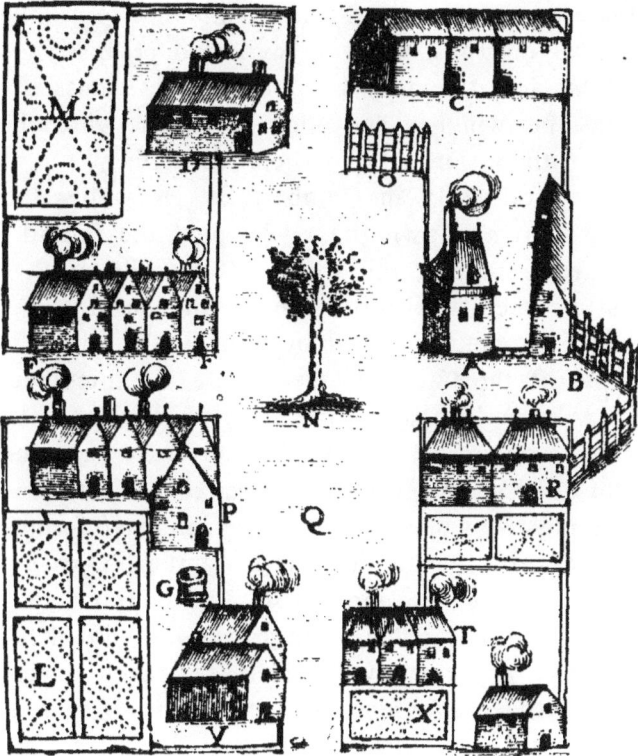

THE HABITATION AT ST. CROIX.

A, Dwelling of De Monts. B, Public building. C, Storehouse. D, Guard-house.
E, Blacksmith's shop. F, Carpenters' dwelling. G, Well. L and M, Gardens.
N, Open space. O, Palisade. P, Champlain's house. Q, R, T, Other dwellings.

blacksmith's shop, guard-house and gardens. Besides
these they had built a cook-house and a little chapel
outside the palisade, all of which were defended by a
little fort on which cannon were mounted.

Winter came upon them sooner than they had expected, so they could not accomplish all they intended to do. Still, they had cleared ground for planting, both on the island and the adjacent mainland, and had laid out gardens, and sowed wheat, and had put in other seeds, all of which came up well, and promised a good yield. At low tide they gathered cockles, mussels, sea-urchins, periwinkles, and other shell-fish, which helped to make their store of provisions go farther.

Snow fell early in October. By December the ice began floating down the river, past the island. The cold grew sharper, the springs froze, the north wind whistled keen and chill through the chinks of their rudely built cottages. And by and by the snow fell to a depth of three to four feet, while the thick ice that formed everywhere about the shores kept them prisoners on their solitary island. Winter had come in earnest.

But a worse enemy than cold seized one after another; for during the winter scurvy in a malignant form broke out and rapidly reduced their number. Day by day matters grew worse and worse. The colonists did not know what this terrible scourge was, nor did their surgeon have any remedy for it. So it raged unchecked until out of seventy-nine men in all thirty-five fell victims to the dread disease. Those who were attacked grew so weak that they were unable to rise, or move, or even to be helped upon their feet without fainting and falling to the ground. All this suffering and death was caused by being compelled to live on salted meat, having no fruits or vegetables, and little else for food. They were like sailors at sea, cut off from all intercourse with the world and perishing for the want of fresh provisions.

During this period of extreme cold all their liquors froze except the Spanish wine, for their houses had been hastily built without cellars to store their food supplies in. Their cider had to be chopped up and served out like ice by the pound. For want of good water they melted snow and drank it, as they could not get to the mainland because of the ice piled about the shores of the island. For the same reason they also suffered for want of firewood, there being few trees on the island; so that even with the forests all around them they could not have warm fires, but were compelled to economize their fuel to the detriment of their sick people. And this hardship added to their suffering.

INDIAN HUNTER ON SNOW-SHOES.

They had a hand-mill for grinding wheat, but the few who were not actually prostrated with sickness were too weak to operate it. And these few had to tend the sick and take care of the dying, as well as do all the necessary work, the saddest of which was digging graves for their comrades in the frozen ground.

So they passed through all the horrors of an arctic winter, as far from civilization and the help of their friends as if a frozen ocean were between them.

These misfortunes caused great discontent. The gay and light-hearted Frenchmen of De Monts' company were cast down by them, and they were eager to leave the plague-stricken place. De Monts himself shared this feeling in common with his companions. He had not counted on six months of winter — and such a winter! The pleasant summer had deceived them. Like an enchantress, it had lured them to their ruin.

In March some savages made their way to the island with game, which they had killed. This was the life these people led in winter. It was their only means of subsistence. In summer they fished, in winter they hunted, but did not cultivate the soil. For their meat the French gave the Indians bread and such other things as they could spare.

The French found that these Indians had been hunting the elk, moose and deer; and that to keep from sinking in the deep snow they put on very large snow-shoes,[13] with which they could walk very rapidly, and easily overtake the animals they pursued, floundering in the snow as if sunk in the mire. Women and children wore snow-shoes like the hunters and were very expert in the use of them. When the Indians came upon the track of a wild animal they followed it up as swiftly as possible until they got near enough to shoot it with their arrows or pierce it with their spears; for so heavy a creature as the elk or moose would soon become exhausted by its struggles to escape. Then the women and children would come up, scrape off the snow, build a hut, light great fires, and all would feast as long as the venison lasted. Then to the hunt again.

De Monts looked for his vessels back from France by the end of April. As they did not come he determined to get ready his small bark and go to the river St. Lawrence for help. Before he could do this, however, a vessel arrived at the settlement, to the great joy of the survivors who remained to welcome her. De Monts now determined to seek a better place of settlement than this in which he had passed so miserable a winter. With this purpose the bark was manned and victualled and taking Champlain with him they set out on the 18th of June, 1605, to explore the coasts beyond.

After carefully searching all the harbors as far as Cape Cod, where the natives treacherously slew one of his men, without finding a place to his liking, De Monts returned to St. Croix. Fully determined not to pass another winter there he forthwith removed his people to Port Royal, in Nova Scotia, and so was ended disastrously the second attempt to plant a colony in New England.

[1] DE MONTS, Pierre du Guast, a native of the province of Saintonge in France. Officer of the king's household. He was a Huguenot, or French Protestant. He had already been in Canada and knew something of the country and its resources.

[2] NEW FRANCE. This name is on all old maps made after the discoveries of Verrazano. Afterwards given to all the French possessions in North America.

[3] THE BEST POINT, for settlement. We see the same idea actuating both French and English at this time— namely, a site somewhere in the latitude of New England.

[4] GOOD AND BAD. De Monts had authority to take, at need, convicts from the prisons in order to fill up his complement of men.

[5] CHAMPLAIN was a native of the same province as De Monts, his patron. He served in the civil wars, learned navigation and drawing, and had been in Canada, Mexico and the West Indies. In these voyages he had acquired much information of value to his patron. Champlain was a man of sterling worth, a keen observer, an accomplished geographer, a good comrade, added to which the qualities of courage and persistency among reverses gave him a commanding influence in the affairs of New France. He made the first authentic map of New England and the drawing given on page 25 is from his hand. He was the founder of Quebec, the discoverer of Lake Champlain and the historian of his time.

[6] PASSAMAQUODDY BAY(Indian)Eastern coast of Maine. Partly British water. The St. Croix River flows into the head of it.

[7] ST. CROIX (French for Holy Cross) now De Monts Island. Called Holy Cross because two streams entered the river here, giving it the form of a cross. The name since transferred to the river, which was first called Etchemins from the natives inhabiting its shores. Eastern boundary of the United States.

[8] MONTS DÉSERTS (French for Desert Mountains). The name is now used in the singular as Mt. Desert. Indian name Pemetiq—meaning the head or—"the place which is at the head."

[9] PENTEGOUET or PENTAGOUET (Indian). Called by the English Penobscot at a very early day and indicating different ways of pronouncing the Indian name, which signifies a place where there are rapids, or a stony place.

[10] FALLS, near the city of Bangor.

[11] NOROMBEGA. This story is traced back to an anonymous relation of 1539, which says the natives called their country Norombega. But André Thévet says he was there in 1556, and that the natives called it "Agoncy." Refer to p. 4.

[12] ISLE AU HAUT (French for High Island) situated at the entrance to Penobscot Bay.

[13] SNOW-SHOES (French, Raquettes). To an oval frame of hard wood, strengthened with cross-pieces, the Indians fastened a meshwork made of animal intestines, in the manner of a tennis-raquet or battledore. There was a socket at one end to receive the toe; and thongs at the other secured the snow-shoe to the wearer's ankle.

POPHAM COLONY, 1607.

TWENTY-THREE years had passed since the granting of Raleigh's almost royal privileges, yet no Englishman occupied a foot of New England soil. Elizabeth was dead, James reigned in England, Raleigh was a prisoner in the Tower.

DISCOVERY CROSS.

Undismayed by previous failures, each of which seems providentially paving the way to final success, the great or little personages, whose interests or ambitions were bound up in colonization, straightway began laying their plans for a new trial.

One strong motive to these efforts, if not the strongest, came from the reports brought by Gosnold concerning the copper possessed by the Indians. Since they had it, rich mines[1] of this metal must exist somewhere in the country.

That seemed clear. To find these mines, to get and ship the ores back to England, was the controlling purpose with the men who equipped this colony. They hoped for some such gains as the Spaniards were reaping from the mines of Mexico which were the talk of all Europe.

Should they succeed, it would not benefit England any the less on that account because the new country would be peopled.

Great opportunity for wealth was then the alluring prize set before the ambitious and adventurous spirits of the time.[2]

As the best means for effecting the desired object a division

SAGADAHOC, OR KENNEBEC.

of Virginia and a division of effort were called for. This, it was thought, would promote healthy rivalry. Raleigh's privileges were therefore set aside. In their stead James now granted charters to two great companies, one of them called the London Company,[3] the other the Plymouth Company,[4] and Virginia was divided in nearly equal portions between them.

Sir John Popham, Lord Chief Justice of England,[5] was the master spirit of the Plymouth Company. He

and his associates made ready two vessels, one being commanded by his kinsman, George Popham, the other by Raleigh Gilbert, which, with a hundred and twenty persons sailed from Plymouth in June 1607 for the river Sagadahoc,[6] in North Virginia.

Where was this river Sagadahoc? and how came it to be chosen to begin a settlement at?

After Gosnold's return to England some of those who had helped to fit him out succeeded in enlisting Thomas Arundel, Baron of Wardour, in the good work that Gosnold had begun. This nobleman had fitted out a ship which sailed for Virginia on Easter Sunday 1605.[7] George Weymouth was its commander. He made his first land in the latitude of Cape Cod, whence he was driven by contrary winds as far up the coast as the mouth of a fine river, which he carefully sounded and explored for many leagues. In token of possession he caused his men to set up crosses with the king's arms thereon at different points, according to the usage of civilized nations.[8]

Like Gosnold, Weymouth took careful note of every thing he saw. His men caught great cod four and five feet long, over the ship's side, as fast as they could bait hooks. They took lobsters in the same way. They found the land well-timbered with great forests, well-watered with sweet streams, well-stocked with game, and they judged it by the trial of a few seeds abundantly fruitful for all kinds of English grain. In a word, they found Gosnold's reports to be true in every particular.

Weymouth had been told to bring some of the natives home to England. To this end he used great friendliness toward them. He tried to get their confidence, and lull any suspicions they might have of his intentions. He also tried to make them believe that the whites were superior beings, and this was the way he took to prove it to them. One day when he was going among them Weymouth rubbed the steel blade of his sword with a loadstone. Having done this he astonished the ignorant natives by taking up a knife with his sword, making the knife follow the point around as he held the sword near it, or with other equally simple experiments.

But the natives were suspicious—so much so that Weymouth finally had to kidnap five of them, not being able to entice so many on board his ship at once. With these he set sail for England.

As those who had sent him meant to reap for themselves whatever advantage the voyage might bring, they kept the knowledge of the place where Weymouth had been to themselves. But the arrival of the five Indians,[9] together with the glowing reports spread abroad by Weymouth's men, gave to the cause of colonization a fresh impulse throughout the kingdom.

Weymouth called the river he had discovered the Sagadahoc. He gave a glowing account of it. By his report it wanted nothing to render it a most desirable place to settle a colony in. A bold coast, a harbor in which the royal navy might safely ride, fresh-water springs, fine timber trees, fish and game in great abundance, with a navigable river stretching a highway for commerce with the natives far into the interior, were the features of Sagadahoc as Weymouth described them. During his brief stay he had made trial with a few seeds of the soil and had found it to promise a good harvest. He had found the simple natives willing to give a beaver-skin in return for things of little or no value. Altogether Weymouth's account was quite as favorable as Gosnold's.

Popham's colonists purposed making their settlement in this river: and one of the Indians that Weymouth had carried off was sent back with them to be their interpreter, and tell of the greatness of England. The two ships, the "Mary and John" and the "Gift of God," got sight of the coast on the 30th of July. Night fell before they could reach it, so the sails were furled and the ships lay to until morning. The next day they stood

[FORT POPHAM.]APPROACH TO THE KENNEBEC.[SEGUIN ISLAND.]

in for the shore and dropped anchor [10] under shelter of a large island.

Their first greeting was to come as Gosnold's had from a boat-load of savages who, after paddling round the ship, but at a safe distance, were finally persuaded to come on board. These Indians also had a boat of the same kind as that first seen on this coast by Gosnold. [11]

From this place the colonists sailed south-west, as they found the coast to run in that direction, until they had brought Weymouth's landmarks to bear correctly from the ship. Again they let go their anchor under the lee of another large island, [12] for the voyage was now completed.

Skit'war'res, one of the Indians whom Weymouth had kidnapped, was on board Captain Gilbert's ship. Taking Skitwarres along with him Gilbert manned his boat and went on shore, at Pemaquid,[13] where the Indians had a village. Upon Gilbert's approach these Indians at first ran to their arms with loud cries; but on seeing Skitwarres in company with the English they became pacified, and welcomed the new-comers hospitably.

On Sunday Captain Popham and Captain Gilbert, with nearly all their people, landed upon the island where Captain Weymouth's cross stood, and heard a sermon preached by their chaplain.

> "They bade the holy dews of prayer
>   Baptize a heathen sod:
> And 'mid the groves a church arose
>   Unto the Christian's God." [14]

This day, the 9th of August, 1607, marks the first formal observance of Christian worship on New England soil that is distinctly mentioned.[15]

Some time was spent in exploring. It was the middle of August before the colonists entered the Sagadahoc which they knew by Sat'quin,[16] the island at its mouth. Choice was made of a site to begin settlement at the mouth of the river.[17]   On the 19th all went on shore, and after hearing a sermon, the president's commission was read to the assembled colonists.

Work now began in earnest. It was the lovely season of early autumn. While some cleared away the underbrush, carried earth, or helped to frame the first houses, others brought stores from the ships, went to the woods or labored in other ways. They first began building a storehouse and fort, as Gosnold and De Monts had done before them. While this was in progress the shipwrights were set to work building a pinnace [18] for the colonists' use.

Before cold weather set in all had worked so diligently that they had finished their fort, mounted twelve cannons upon its walls, completed the storehouse, erected a chapel, and had built fifty cabins besides. Their pin-

AN EXPLORING PARTY.

nace was called Virginia in compliment to the country in which it was the first vessel to be built.

While this habitation was daily growing up out of the wilderness, Captain Gilbert was actively searching the seacoast, both east and west, as well as the river itself. For a while the Indians seemed distrustful, and held aloof, but curiosity at length so far overcame their fears that numbers came to see what the white men were doing in that place.

These Indians differed little in appearance from those Gosnold had seen and described. If any thing they were men of somewhat larger frame than those farther south.

Their bows were made of witch-hazel or beech, their arrows and spears headed with a sharp bone, or the pointed tail of the horseshoe-crab. In the use of both weapons they were very dexterous indeed, seldom missing a deer with the one or failing to strike a salmon with the other.

Knowing this the English always wore their armor [19] when making excursions by land or water, nor did they ever feel quite safe, although besides his steel cap and corselet, the explorer usually carried a target in addition to his musket, his rest, and his sword. Loaded down with all these arms rapid movement was impossible and quick firing equally so. [20]

FOOT SOLDIER OF 1607.

More than once the Indians seemed almost to have made up their minds to attack the intruders. They remembered the treachery of Weymouth. But their fear of the English firearms was so great, and the chances of open combat so unequal, that they sought for an opportunity to take

the white men at a disadvantage, or by using stratagem
to put them off their guard. This was the Indian's
method of making war. No man braver than he, but it
was his maxim never to run any risk if he could possibly
avoid it. To steal unperceived upon his adversary was
the art of war, as his fathers had taught it to him and
as they had learned it from the panther, the catamount
and the wild-cat of the woods.

They were crafty fellows, these Indians. Once while
Gilbert was making a boat journey up the river he came
to an Indian encampment. The savages were all armed
and painted as if going to battle. They pretended to
a willingness for trade, but only as a cloak, for one of
them having got into the boat he suddenly snatched up
the firebrand, always kept for lighting the slow-matches
and flung it into the water. He then leaped after it and
struck out for the shore. Some of his comrades then
seized the boat-rope and held it fast, while others fitted
their arrows as if going to shoot. Gilbert's men instantly
pointed their muskets at them, which, though rendered
useless for the moment, caused the Indians such fear
that they gave up the contest and went off into the
woods.

Such experiences as this convinced the English that
the savages were no contemptible adversaries and they
wisely did every thing to keep peace between them.

The winter was very cold—much colder than the
colonists had imagined it would be and much longer.
In the course of it their president fell ill and died. A
few others also fell victims to disease, but on the whole,
this settlement fared much better than its French prede-
cessor at St. Croix had done. In the spring Captain
Davis arrived with a plentiful supply of arms, tools,

victuals, and every thing necessary for the subsistence of the plantation, but its fate was already decided. Hearing by this ship that his brother whose heir he was had died and that Lord Popham, their noble patron, was also dead, Gilbert would not consent to remain longer in the country. The plantation being thus deprived of its head, with homesickness and discontent every day increasing, it was speedily decided to give over the attempt to remain in the country. The decision was immediately carried out.

ARROW-HEAD
(actual size).

FLINT ARROW-HEAD
(actual size).

[1] MINES. De Monts brought an experienced miner from France. One of the very first things he did was to send this man, with Champlain, to find the mines of which he had heard report.

[2] EXAGGERATED REPORTS had undoubtedly spread over Europe.

[3] LONDON COMPANY, because formed of noblemen and merchants of London. This company took the south half, or South Virginia.

[4] PLYMOUTH COMPANY. Similarly formed at Bristol, Plymouth etc. This company took the northern half, extending from Pennsylvania to Nova Scotia.

[5] SIR JOHN POPHAM died this same year, 1607.

[6] SAGADAHOC (Indian). From the meeting of the Kennebec and Androscoggin rivers to the sea. Champlain says, the Indians called it Quinibequy, which has been construed into Kennebec and is the name now generally ac-

cepted for the whole course of the greater river to the sea. In Indian the mouth of the river.

[7] EASTER. The festival observed by Christians in commemoration of the resurrection of Our Lord.

[8] CROSSES OF SOVEREIGNTY. The universal Christian symbol, denoting first, possession by Christian people, secondly, sovereignty assumed in the name of the particular discoverer's prince, to be evidence to all who came after.

[9] WEYMOUTH'S INDIANS. Note that they were seen on their arrival by Sir F. Gorges, who then commanded at Plymouth, England.

[10] DROPPED ANCHOR; cables of hemp were then used.

[11] I wish constantly to impress the fact that as early as this seems to us, fishing-ships were here much earlier.

[12] MONHEGAN ISLAND. Weymouth

had set up a cross on it and called it St. George's Island. The earliest frequented fishing-station of the New England coast.

[13] PEMAQUID. The peninsula on the mainland nearest to Monhegan and twelve miles distant. Now in Bristol, Me. Also the river entering the peninsula on the east.

[14] MRS. LYDIA H. SIGOURNEY is the author.

[15] FIRST CHRISTIAN WORSHIP, Yet as De Monts had his curate at St. Croix and had also built a chapel there, it would seem that Christian worship may have been first held there.

[16] SATQUIN (Indian) corrupted into Seguin. The island-landmark of the Kennebec lying between Cape Small Point and Georgetown. It shows a light 200 feet above the sea.

[17] FORT POPHAM, named by the government for this colony, now marks the site. A memorial stone with this in-scription has been placed within the walls of the fort:

THE FIRST COLONY
ON THE SHORES OF NEW ENGLAND
WAS FOUNDED HERE.
AUGUST 19TH, O.S. 1607
UNDER
GEORGE POPHAM.

[OLD STYLE, here first referred to, continued in use until 1752. The new year began March 25th.]

[18] PINNACE, a small vessel with sails and oars, suitable for coasting where larger crafts could not go.

[19] ARMOR, a steel cuirass covering the wearer's breast and back, sometimes made in two parts, and laced together under the arms.

[20] MUSKET-FIRING. A cannon can now be loaded and fired in less time than the muskets of that time could be. A soldier had to lay his musket in the rest, pour in the priming, and touch it off with his slow-match, carried for the purpose in a long coil.

DISCOVERY OF LAKE CHAMPLAIN, 1609.

THOUGH baffled in his first attempts De Monts never theless resolved to persevere.[1]

This time he determined to direct his efforts to the St. Lawrence, but instead of going himself, he despatched the trusty Champlain thither, as his lieutenant.

Champlian again left France in April, 1608. He entered the St. Lawrence in May, sailed up this great river as far as a place which the Indians called Quebec,[2] and then and then and there laid the foundations of the city which was to be the great stronghold and key of Canada.

The Canadian winter was cruel. But nobly did Champlain fulfil the expectations of De Monts. Spring having come at last Champlain set out in June on a tour of exploration higher up the river, which the Indians had told him came from the country of the redoubtable and warlike Ir´o´quois.[3]

While on his way Champlain met with two or three hundred Hu´ron and Al´gon´-quin [4] warriors who prayed Champlain to help them fight the Iroquois, their deadly enemies. Champlain promised to do so, and to please his savage allies he caused muskets and arquebuses to be fired which made them give loud cries of astonishment.

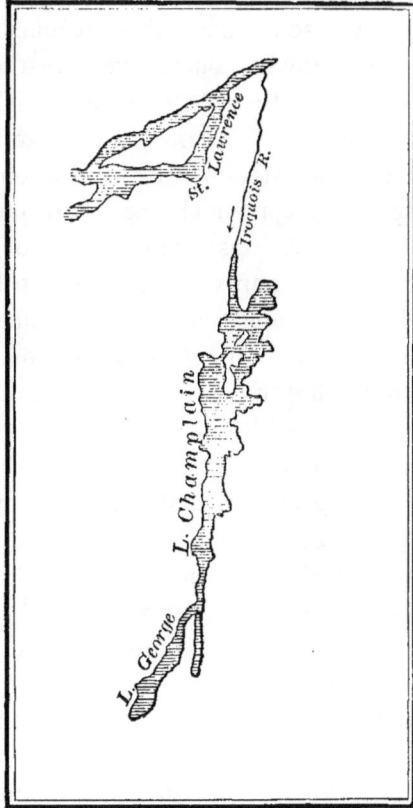

CHAMPLAIN'S ROUTE.

These Indians having entreated Champlain to go back with them to the French settlement, in order that they might see the houses, he thought it best to gratify them. Accordingly, they all returned to Quebec where the Indians spent several days in dancing and feasting as was their custom before going to war.

When this was over all again set out for the land of the Iroquois, Champlain in his shallop, the Hurons and Algonquins in their canoes.

After some days they reached the river of the Iroquois,[5] flowing out of the great lake which the Hurons said was filled with beautiful islands and bordered by pleasant lands where their enemies dwelt.

Up this stream they rowed on until they came to a rapid through which the boats could not pass. The bed of the river was strewn with rocks and shallow places. Finding it impracticable to get his shallop further on Champlain took the heroic resolution of sending it back to Quebec with all but two of his men. Telling the others that by God's grace he would soon return to them he boldly committed himself to the guidance of the Hurons.

The savages passed the rapid by carrying their canoes, their baggage, and their arms through the woods until they reached the head of it. They then launched their canoes and again embarked.

After paddling some leagues further the savages drew their canoes together at the shore. All then landed and began to make a camp for the night. This was done with surprising celerity. Some set to work felling trees for a barricade,[6] some stripping off bark to cover their cabins, and some went forth to see if any enemies were lurking near the encampment, for the allies had now entered the country of the Iroquois.

The Hurons were accompanied by their soothsayer, or medicine-man, whom they believed was able to invoke spirits, for the purpose of finding out whether his tribe would be victorious or not. This Indian sorcerer would go into his hut, fall flat on the ground and begin his invocation to the Evil Spirit, while all the other Indians, squatted like apes around the outside of the medicine lodge, eagerly watched for some sign of their demon's presence to be manifested to them. After lying prostrate a while the soothsayer would suddenly start to his feet and begin a variety of strange antics, violently leaping, and twisting his body with sudden contortions, and also tossing his arms wildly in the air, until the perspiration covered his naked body from head to foot. Then he would speak in a strange voice which his companions believed was the spirit talking, and to which they all listened in great fear.[7]

Champlain believed this soothsayer to be an impostor, but no Indians would go into battle till they had first gone through the ceremony we have described. After hearing the medicine-man's prediction they would practise all the manœuvres they meant to perform in the coming conflict, as soldiers sometimes do in a sham fight.

In two days more Champlain reached the great lake which no Christian had ever seen before him. High mountains [8] rose in the east and south. The Indians paddled swiftly on over the calm surface of the lake. They told Champlain that their enemies dwelt at the foot of the southernmost mountains, but to get there it would be necessary to pass a fall which led to a second lake,[9] nine or ten leagues long. From the foot of this last lake they said it was only a short march to a river [10] which flowed into the sea. In this way Champlain first learned of the great inland highway stretching from the St. Lawrence to the Atlantic.

As the allies drew nearer to the abode of their enemies they travelled only by night, keeping close during
the day. And as the doing so would expose them to
the risk of discovery they could neither hunt nor make
fires to cook their meat, so that a little meal, thiekened
with water, was their only food at such times.

At this time the savages would often ask Champlain
if he had dreamed a dream.[11]   One night he did dream
that he saw all the Iroquois drowning in the lake.
When he had wished to rescue them the Hurons had
prevented him, saying the Iroquois were good-for-
nothing fellows who richly deserved drowning. When
Champlain told his dream the Hurons considered it a
good omen for them and no longer had any doubt that
they would conquer the Iroquois.

Soon after this the Iroquois were met coming up the
lake in their canoes. They had come to fight. As
night was drawing on both parties agreed to wait until
morning before engaging in combat. The Hurons kept
the lake in their canoes, the Iroquois went on shore and
securely barricaded themselves against attack. In order
that they might not get scattered during the night the
Hurons fastened their canoes together with poles, with
in arrow-shot of the Iroquois camp.

The night was passed on both sides in singing war-
songs and bandying defiances or insults to and fro; for
with all their bravery the Indians were great braggarts.
The Iroquois warriors told the Hurons that they were
all cowards and would see what would happen so soon
as there was light enough. The Hurons were not behind in retorting in a like strain.

When it was day the Iroquois, near two hundred
strong, sallied forth out of their barricade, and after

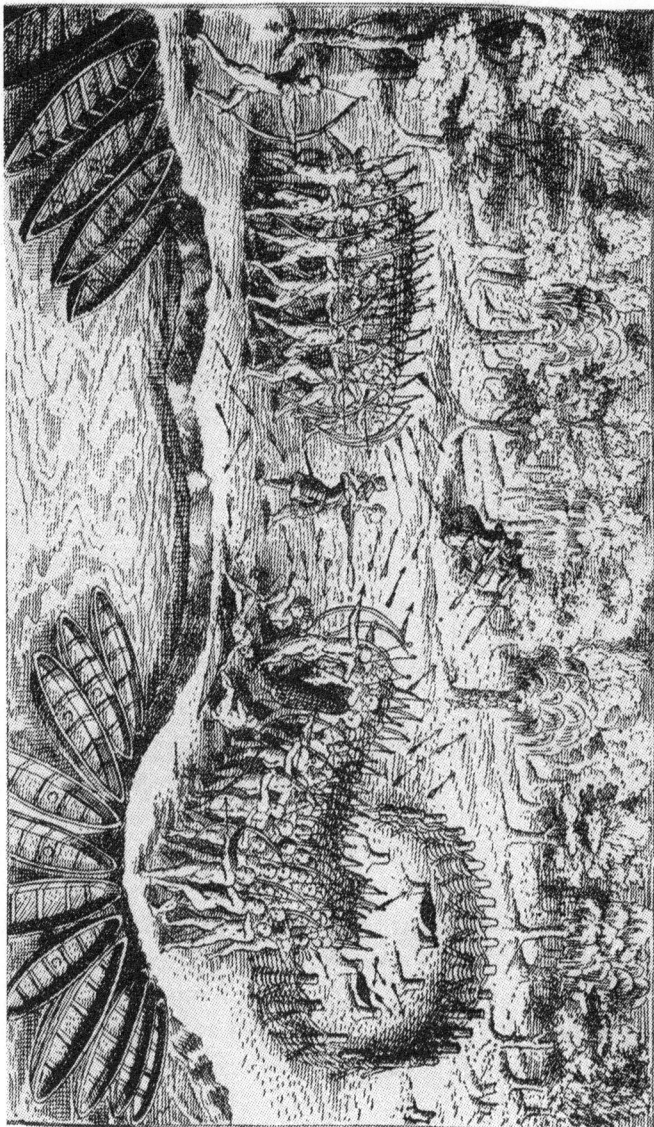

THE BATTLE AT LAKE CHAMPLAIN. - DRAWN BY CHAMPLAIN.

forming in battle order, marched slowly, but with a bold front, toward their adversaries who had landed and were waiting for them. Three war chiefs, distinguished by flowing plumes, led the Iroquois into battle. Seeing them thus come on in splendid array the Hurons seemed struck with fear for they loudly called on Champlain to lead them. So Champlain went through their ranks and out into the open space between them and their enemies to within thirty paces of the Iroquois whom he faced with his arquebuse ready in his hand.

On perceiving him the Iroquois halted and gazed as if wondering who and what this strange being could be who seemed without fear. Presently recovering from their surprise the Iroquois bent their bows and made ready to send a flight of arrows among the Hurons. Champlain raised his arquebuse to his shoulder. Aiming straight at an Iroquois chief he fired. His shot carried dismay into the Iroquois ranks. Never before had these savages witnessed the dreadful power of the white man's firearms. Three Iroquois fell, one wounded mortally, two killed outright. Seeing this execution done among them in an instant the rest stood dismayed and irresolute while the Hurons raised loud and exultant cries of victory.

For a moment the Iroquois braves did not seem to know what had killed their comrades, but they soon renewed the battle with a volley of arrows.

Notwithstanding the odds against them the Iroquois fought bravely on until one of Champlain's men fired upon them from an ambush which again threw them into disorder. They then broke and fled in terror, abandoning their camp to the victors.

Champlain pursued them into the woods, killing still

more of them. The Hurons also killed several and took ten or twelve prisoners. Fifteen or sixteen of the allies were wounded, but none fatally.

After this victory, the Hurons took a great quantity of corn which the Iroquois had left behind. They also stripped the slain of their arms and armor.[12] They then celebrated their victory with songs of triumph and with feasting after which they reëmbarked with the prisoners they had taken.

Toward nightfall the Indians again landed. Champlain saw that something was intended. Taking one of the prisoners they made a speech to him in which they upbraided him with the cruelties his people had practised toward theirs who had been taken in war. They then told him to sing his death-song if he had the courage.[13] The Iroquois did as he was bid, but his song was a sad one.

While he was doing this his captors had kindled a fire. Each one then plucked out a burning brand with which he proceeded to scorch the victim's naked flesh cruelly. This was done to make him cry out with pain, so that the Hurons might exult over him and say he was a squaw and no warrior. They then tore out his nails, scalped [14] him, and otherwise mutilated the poor wretch until Champlain begged the Hurons to let him shoot the Iroquois warrior and so end his sufferings at once. After he was dead the Hurons cut out his heart and gave a piece of it to his own brother to eat.

Notwithstanding all his dreadful sufferings, we are told that the Iroquois behaved with great fortitude. To show weakness in the presence of his enemies would have brought dishonor upon his whole nation. So Indian stoicism has passed into a proverb.

Now from Champlain's having thoughtlessly taken part in this invasion of the Iroquois country came a war which lasted more than a hundred years, because the Iroquois ever after looked upon the French as their enemies.

The lake where the battle was fought was called by him Lake Champlain. [15]

[1] DE MONTS' patent had been revoked through the efforts of rivals in France. He obtained a new one, running only one year.

[2] QUEBEC. Said to mean in the Algonquin tongue a narrowing, or contraction, and in this connection referring to the narrowing of the river St. Lawrence. Doubtful.

[3] IROQUOIS COUNTRY is now included in the State of New York. Called Iroquois by the French but generally known to the English as Five Nations, viz. Mohawks, Oneidas, Onondagas, Cayugas, Senecas. They became allies of the English.

[4] HURONS, or WYANDOTS, were originally from the region bordering on Lake Huron; ALGONQUINS from that north of the St. Lawrence and east of Lake Huron. These tribes came under French control.

[5] IROQUOIS RIVER, so-called because it led to the country of the Iroquois. Afterward Sorel, now Richelieu River.

[6] BARRICADE, what would now be called an *abatis* (French) in war. In thus protecting their camps by intrenchments the Indians followed a custom of the ancient Romans which is also practised by civilized nations to-day.

[7] MEDICINE-MAN. In Cooper's "Leather-Stocking Tales," the doings of these Indian magicians are well described. I commend these books for their generally accurate delineation of Indian manners.

[8] GREEN MOUNTAINS AND ADIRONDACK MOUNTAINS.

[9] LAKE GEORGE.

[10] HUDSON RIVER.

[11] DREAMS AND OMENS. All Indians put great faith in them. An evil omen commonly turned them from a design.

[12] INDIAN ARMOR. Champlain says the Iroquois wore light armor of wood, interwoven with cotton yarn so as to make it arrow-proof.

[13] DEATH SONG. A chant in which the victim casted of his exploits, mocked his enemies, threatened them with the vengeance of his people and invoked the aid of the Great Spirit.

[14] SCALPING, by drawing a knife, in a circle, around the crown of the head, so that a portion of the scalp could be torn from it. As it was considered a proof of his prowess no Indian ever omitted to secure his enemy's scalp. He would do any thing to prevent his enemy from getting possession of it. The tuft of hair, or topknot, which every Indian wore was called the scalp-lock, and usually decorated with eagles' or hawks' feathers. When a war-party entered their village the scalps were carried suspended to a pole, in triumph.

[15] LAKE CHAMPLAIN. This lake makes for its entire length the boundary between Vermont and New York. Champlain had thus established the extreme southeast and northwest boundaries of New England as well as first explored nearly its whole seacoast.

INDIAN LEGENDS,—ORIGIN OF THE EARTH AND OF MAN.

NEARLY all of the Algonquin tribes gave the sovereign spirit, whom they believed to have created all things, the name of Michabou or the Great Hare. Their fathers had told them that while Michabou with his court of quadrupeds was one day taking his pleasure abroad upon the waters, which then covered the whole world, he formed the earth of a single grain of sand, taken from the bottom of the ocean. Michabou then made men from the dead bodies of animals, found floating upon the the waters. So we see the modern idea of "evolution" first presented in the

INDIAN VILLAGE.

traditions of the ancient races of this continent, with the difference that to the Indian God was always the Creator.

The tradition of the Iroquois was even more curious. It was to the effect that the King of Heaven being one day greatly provoked with his wife had cast her headlong from heaven to earth. A solitary turtle happened to be swimming upon the waves of the Great Deluge when this took place. The Queen of Heaven fell without hurt upon the turtle's back and so was saved from drowning. In a little time, the waters having subsided, the turtle swam with his burden to the dry land and laid it at the foot of a tree where the rescued woman soon gave birth to twins. But the oldest son soon killed his brother in order that he might inherit the whole earth.

In this tradition we not only have the story of the Great Deluge, which in one form or another appears in most Indian lore, but also that of Cain and Abel as resulting from the woman's expulsion from Eden. Similarly, the turtle supplies the place of the Ark in this legend.

Another Algonquin legend says that after God had destroyed every living thing by the Deluge he sent a raven to explore the abyss of waters. The bird went forth but came back without bringing any tidings from the earth. He then sent a muskrat on the same errand with better success, for this intelligent animal brought back in its paws a little earth out of which the God created a new world. He shot arrows into the naked trunks of such trees as the Deluge had spared, and they sprouted into green branches, and the branches put forth leaves.

HURON TOTEM.

Afterward, in order to repeople the earth, the Spirit took for his wife a female muskrat, by whom he had children.

All these legends tended to strengthen the Indian's

veneration for the higher species of animals, such as the beaver, the bear and the fox, in all of which he saw something like human intelligence. The beaver was wise, the hare swift, the fox cunning, the bear uncon querable. Therefore some tribes adopted an animal as their badge, or totem, under which they fought and by which they were known, just as the knights of old were distinguished by the particular device borne on their shields.

———————

THE COLONY OF MADAME DE GUERCHEVILLE, 1613.

THE Sieur De Monts had given his town of Port Royal, which he had founded after breaking up at St. Croix, to his friend and companion the Sieur De Pou'-trin'court.[1] King Henry IV. had graciously confirmed the right of the Sieur De Poutrincourt therein.

So far, the fur-trade had been the sole object which the patrons of the French colonists had kept in view. Neither agriculture nor the fisheries were promoted. Trade, and trade only, was looked to as the chief resource of New France.

King Henry now gave Poutrincourt notice that it was time to do something for the conversion of the Indians of Acadie. He made known his wish that some Jesuit[2] fathers should go there as missionaries.

This step was productive of the most important results to all Canada, or New France, in which, as we have said, Acadie was included.

Many of the Jesuit fathers accordingly volunteered to go to Acadie, but two only, Fathers Biard and Masse, were chosen.

Before they could embark, Henry had been stabbed

in the streets of Paris by the fanatic Ravaillac. And his death put an end to the hopes of the Sieur De Monts, because the Catholic party were now in control and he was a Protestant.

Madame De Guercheville,[3] a noble Catholic lady of the court, had taken the cause of this mission to Acadie much to heart. But for reasons of his own Poutrincourt did not want the Jesuits to gain a foothold in his colony at all and he accordingly threw many obstacles in the way of their going. But they finally went.

MOUNT DESERT ISLAND.

At last Madame De Guercheville resolved to fit out a vessel herself, and become the patron of a new colony. Other court ladies helped her. She ordered the commander, La Saus'saye, to provide every thing requisite for beginning a new colony which was meant to be settled in the Penobscot River. No doubt the choice was determined by the reports of De Monts and Champlain on their return to France. It was, moreover, outside the jurisdiction of Poutrincourt at Port Royal. It was to be an original colony with a religious foundation.

These colonists numbered in all about thirty persons, including two other Jesuit fathers, named Jacques Quentin and Gilbert Du Thet.

Upon his arrival with his ship at Port Royal, La Saussaye took the two Jesuit fathers there on board and again made sail for his final destination, hoping as it was at no great distance, to reach it without accident.

"But God," says the pious Biard, "ordered otherwise," for when off Manan' they were enveloped in so thick a fog that day and night were hardly different. For two days and nights they were tossed about at the mercy of the waves. In this extremity the fathers prayed to heaven for help and soon the fog cleared, the stars came out, and before them rose the majestic summits of Mt. Desert to point their way onward.

Their pilot now took them safely into a fine anchorage on the east side of the island, which in joy for their deliverance from shipwreck, they named St. Sauveur,[5] and celebrated with a mass.

Here they met with friendly Indians of whom they inquired their way to their intended place of settlement. These Indians urged them to stay where they were, telling them that it was so pleasant and healthful an abode that when the savages of other places fell sick they were brought to this one to be cured.

Upon viewing the place again, the French colonists decided to go no further. They fixed upon a pretty little hill that sloped gently down to the sea for their settlement. Two pleasant brooks rippled about its base. The harbor was a very fine one—as safe as an inland lake, so deep that the largest ship might lie within a cable's length of the shore, and spacious enough to float a royal fleet.

Having first set up a cross where they landed, the colonists proceeded to pitch their tents and prepare to build houses. A fort was thrown up, as a necessary measure of precaution and protection, and gardens were laid out and every thing done to secure themselves against the season or provide for their sustenance. But they little thought of the foe flying to destroy them.

During this summer of 1613 an armed ship, commanded by Samuel Argall,[6] came from Virginia to this coast on a fishing voyage. Driven eastward by stress of weather Argall heard of the arrival of La Saussaye from the Indians, who supposed him a friend of these colonists. He determined to expel the French as intruders upon his master's dominions.

One day, the unsuspecting settlers at St. Sauveur saw a large ship bearing swiftly down upon them under a press of sail, with ensigns flying, drums beating, and trumpets sounding as if bent upon a warlike encounter. At first the colonists knew not whether this strange bark were friend or foe, but their doubts were soon cleared up for Argall returned their friendly hail with so terrible a broadside of cannon and musketry that the English vessel seemed belching flames from every side. Surprised and overpowered, the French made only the feeblest resistance. Brother Du Thet, indeed, had bravely seized a match, but was shot down in the act of firing a cannon. Some French sailors who were on board a bark lying in the harbor fled in terror to the shore. Two were drowned while trying to reach it. Those on shore made no attempt to defend themselves. A few made their escape. It was a complete surprise and surrender.

SHIP UNDER SAIL

Pretending to believe that the French were free-booters, Argall gave the settlement up to plunder. Some of the prisoners were sent off in a boat to Port Royal, the rest were taken to Virginia. Brother Du Thet was buried by his sorrowing companions at the foot of the cross they had raised when coming to the shore.

In a subsequent voyage Argall destroyed all traces of this settlement. After much searching he found, and also destroyed, the houses at St. Croix which De Monts had left standing on his departure. And thus disastrously ended the attempts of the French to gain a foothold on the soil of New England.

[1] JEAN DE POUTRINCOURT accompanied De Monts to Acadie in 1604. He went back to France in the same ship that brought the colonists over, returned in 1606 as De Monts' lieutenant, and was instrumental in the selection of Port Royal as a place of settlement. By direction of De Monts, Poutrincourt with Champlain continued the exploration along the coast, begun in the previous year. While doing so he had a fight with the Cape Cod Indians, losing four men.

[2] JESUITS, or Society of Jesus. Founded by Ignatius Loyola in 1534. The members were required to take vows of chastity, poverty, obedience and implicit submission to the Holy See. It became so formidable that great efforts were finally made to break it up.

[3] MADAME DE GUERCHEVILLE was aided by the queen-regent, Marie De Medicis.

[4] MANAN, or Grand Manan (Indian Manthane). The large island at the entrance to Passamaquoddy Bay.

[5] ST. SAUVEUR Doubt exists as to the exact locality of this settlement. Tradition fixes it at Fernald's Point, at the southwest entrance to Somes' Sound.

[6] SAMUEL ARGALL was afterward Deputy-governor of Virginia. On his second expedition to Acadie he destroyed Port Royal, now Annapolis, N.S. King James knighted him.

DISCOVERY OF BLOCK ISLAND, 1614.

WHILE the French had been working their way down the coast from the east, the Dutch had been pushing up the coast from the west. Through the solitudes of Lake Champlain, Champlain was nearing the sources of the Hudson from the north when Hendrik Hudson,[1] in searching for a western passage to Cathay,[2]

"That men might quickly sail to India,"

was ascending this noble river from the south.

Hudson went back to Holland to report his discovery to his employers. Shortly after this two Dutch mariners, one of whom was Adrian Block, chartered a ship to go out to this new region, which Hudson praised so highly. Upon their favorable account of it certain merchants of the United Provinces[3] fitted them out for another voyage. Manhattan Island was the appointed rendezvous.

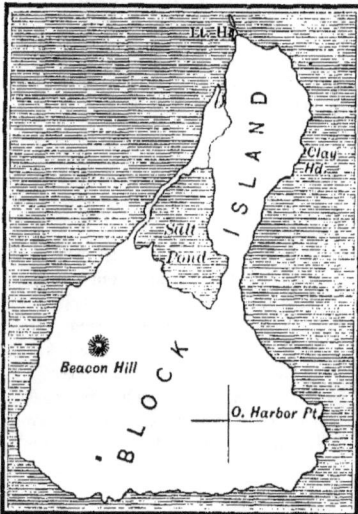

Block's vessel took fire and was burnt at Manhattan by accident. He then built himself a small

BLOCK ISLAND.

yacht, or pinnace, out of timber cut on the island. With this yacht of only sixteen tons burden Block sailed to the eastward, where as yet the larger Dutch ships had not ventured. Sailing boldly through the dangerous "Hell Gate"[4] into Long Island Sound the adventurous Block coasted the shores of this great basin, finding on his way, and ascending for some distance, the beautiful river which the natives called Quoh'neht'a'cut.[5]

Continuing his search Block looked into the Thames, or Pe'quod River, after which he steered across the Sound to Montauk Point. He next visited a large island lying to the northeast of Montauk which on that account has ever since been known as Block Island. [6]

Thence Block went into Narragansett Bay, sailed through the Vineyard Sound in Gosnold's track, doubled

MOHEGAN HEAD, BLOCK ISLAND.

Cape Cod, bringing his voyage in this direction to an end somewhere in Massachusetts Bay, thus overlapping and continuing the explorations that Captain Smith was then making, and of which we will now speak.

> "The island lies nine leagues away.
>   Along its solitary shore,
>   Of craggy rock and sandy bay,
>   No sound but ocean's roar,
> Save where the bold, wild sea-bird makes her home,
> Her shrill cry coming through the sparkling foam."

[1] HENDRIK (Henry) HUDSON, an English navigator in the service of the Dutch East India Company. (*See* Encyc.) His ship, the Half-Moon, left Amsterdam in April 1609. His last voyage was an endeavor to push his way in Cabot's track to India by the far north, this time in the service of English patrons. He was abandoned by his mutinous crew to perish among the ice-fields of the great basin which perpetuates his name, Hudson's Bay.

[2] CATHAY, ancient name for China, and the Land of Spices. To get to the East by sailing to the West was the problem resulting from the discovery that the earth is a globe. It lying in the way, our continent was discovered by accident.

[3] UNITED PROVINCES, united by treaty in 1579 for mutual defence. (*See* art. Holland, Encyc.)

[4] HELL GATE, the narrow strait uniting the waters of the Hudson with Long Island Sound. Originally Helle-gat. So-called from the meeting of opposing tidal currents over submerged rocks, which caused them to boil like a pot. The most dangerous have been removed by blasting, and navigation is nom comparatively safe.

[5] QUOHNEHTACUT (Indian) and Connecticut are the same. The State of Connecticut takes its name from this river.

[6] BLOCK ISLAND is thought to be the one originally discovered by Verrazano and by him named Claudia in honor of the mother of Francis I. It is on many old maps. Indian *Manisses*. Five miles from Point Judith, R.I., to which State the island belongs. *See* "New England Legends."

THE NAMING OF NEW ENGLAND, 1614-1616.

IN the month of April, 1614, some London merchants fitted out two ships for a whaling voyage to North Virginia. They were also to make search for mines of gold and copper. The sending these ships was a strictly business venture having nothing whatever to do with colonization. But much more came of it than its promoters dreamed of.

CAPTAIN JOHN SMITH.

The ships arrived at Monhegan Island. Finding few whales and no gold mines in that neighborhood, they went to fishing at that place, while a boat's crew furnished with trading goods was despatched to open traffic with the natives along the coast.

In this boat went Captain John Smith[1] who was the animating spirit of the whole enterprise. He had never been in this part of Virginia before, but in South, or Old Virginia, he had already had much experience, having served his apprenticeship in that colony, as one might say. First and foremost experience had taught Smith how to deal with the Indians so as to gain their confidence and love. Freely and fearlessly he went among them. At Pemaquid Smith met the great sachem Do'ha'na'da, who was one of those Indians whom Weymouth had carried off to England. Their meeting resulted in Dohanada's inviting Smith to come and live with him and be his ally against his enemies the Tarratines[2] who were allies of the French. And Smith had made up his mind to do this.

Going from place to place Smith traversed the coast as far east as the Penobscot and as far south as Cape Cod. He was a true explorer, for while trading with the Indians he questioned them about the country, the rivers, the coasts, the mountains and of themselves. All that he saw and heard was carefully noted down for future use.

After a stay of three or four months Smith went back to England in one of the ships. What he had seen of the country had decided him to go back again the next year and try his fortunes as a colonist. He made known this determination to Sir Ferdinando Gorges,[3] who encouraged him to persevere in it, and Smith had even gone so far in the matter as to begin recruiting men for his purposed plantation.

Soldier of many wars, traveller in many lands, wise in council as he was valiant in action, of shrewd and

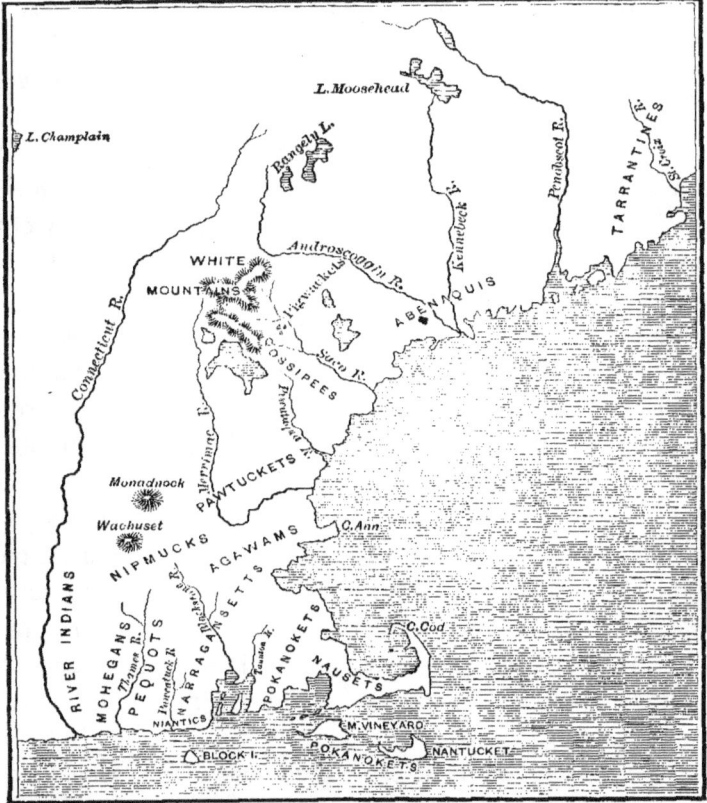

POSITION OF THE NEW ENGLAND TRIBES.

confident nature, resolute and persistent in whatever he undertook, Smith was the very man to have carried his project through against any and every kind of obstacle. In a word he was one of those men who know no such word as fail.

To prevent interference Smith shrewdly kept his destination a secret until he should have matured his plans. He was not destined however to see them happily fulfilled—for though he was so sanguine of success that he was willing to undertake his colony with only sixteen men besides himself, and had been made Admiral[4] of the new country, with power to govern it, he never again set foot on the shores of North Virginia.

Thomas Hunt, master of the other ship, is charged with trying to defeat Smith's purpose, of which he was informed, by awakening the hostility of the Indians towards the English. Smith asserts that Hunt wished to keep the country in the comparative obscurity it then was, to the end that English merchants and masters might exclusively control the fishery and trade as they had been doing.

Being bound for Spain, with his cargo of fish, Hunt stopped at Patuxet[5] and Nauset,[6] where he kidnapped twenty-seven Indians, all of whom he wickedly sold at Malaga to the Spaniards.

With a vessel provided by his friends, Smith again sailed in June 1615, but he and his vessel were taken by pirates, which misadventure brought his voyage to a sudden ending.

So the second attempt to plant a colony under authority of the Plymouth Company fell through. The time had not come for a permanent settlement.

Upon his return to England Smith prepared a map and description of the new country to which he now gave the name of New England.[7] So that in name, at least, the making of New England begins with the voyage and discoveries of Captain John Smith.

Now on Smith's first draught for a map, the Indian names, corresponding with the location of various tribes along the coast, were given. But with more patriotism than foresight Smith had these altered by Prince Charles[8] into English names. His book having been printed before the changes in the map were made we have in one the Indian and on the other the English names.

Let us glance over this map and description and see how far Smith's titles have come down to us.

We will first look up the Indian names because they preserve the history of an extinct people, omitting those that have dropped out of use.

From Penobscot to Cape Cod Smith found at least forty Indian villages and sounded about twenty-five excellent harbors. Beginning with Penobscot, we have Pemaquid, Kennebec, Sagadahoc and Aucocisco (Casco) already named by those who had preceded Smith. Then come Ac'co'min'ti'cus (Ag'amen'ti'cus), Pas'sat'a'-quack (Pis' cat' a' qua), Ag'ga'wom (Ag'a'wam) and Naem'keck (Naum'keag). Then Mat'ta'hunts (Na'-hant) Mas'sa'chu'set,[9] Quon'a'has'sit (Co'has'set) and Nau'set, all of which names were first given by Smith, and have either been retained or are still used as alternates with the English ones.

Now let us turn to the map. We find Cape Elizabeth,[10] Cape Anna [11] and the River Charles [12] laid down on it among a multitude of names that have been superseded by others. All the great bays, nearly all the great rivers except the Merrimack,[13] most of the islands and some of the mountains, as far south as Cape Cod, are more or less accurately represented. Every thing

now included in the States of Rhode Island and Connecticut is left out.

Smith modestly reserved his own name to the little
cluster of islands now known as the Isles of Shoals.
Monhegan, Ma´nan'is, Me'tin'ic, and Ma'tin'i'cus received English names.

One thing about this map of Smith's strikes us very
oddly. It is that while not one solitary white settlement then existed in all New England, most of the
names which Prince Charles gave to savage habitations
were those afterward taken by the later English plantations. Only the locations are different. So that
Smith's map awkwardly and improperly shows a seacoast dotted with English settlements none of which
were even thought of when he made it.

At the close of the year 1616 what had been done
for New England? Its entire seacoast had been explored. Its great bays and rivers had been located and
to some extent surveyed and described. Two maps,
Champlain's and Smith's, gave these discoveries to the
world, with proximate faithfulness. The names and
abodes of the native tribes, their habits and manners,
their numbers and disposition, had been set forth in
sufficient detail for practical men to understand. The
resources of the country,—the fishery, the fur-trade,
the ship-timber, the soil, the natural vegetation and
productions—had been not only often described, but
frequently exhibited in the ports of England, France
and Spain. The route was well known. A thousand
sailors had traversed it. Practical men could now act
intelligently. Finally the name typical of national
sovereignty and national character was of hopeful
augury for the future of New England.

[1] CAPTAIN JOHN SMITH had been a soldier in the Low Countries and in Transylvania, where he was captured by the Turks and sent to Constantinople as a slave. He killed his master and escaped. He went to Virginia in 1606 and to him more than any one was owing the successful founding of that colony.

[2] TARRATINES were Indians dwelling beyond the Penobscot.

[3] SIR FERDINANDO GORGES was governor of Plymouth, Eng., when Weymouth returned from New England with the natives he had stolen. From this circumstance came Gorges' participation in colonizing New England. Upon the division of Virginia he became one of the most active members of the Plymouth Company. Gorges obtained a new charter in 1620 from which came all the later grants of New England.

[4] ADMIRAL; implying control by land and sea.

[5] PATUXET (Indian),   Plymouth.

[6] NAUSET (Indian),   Eastham.

[7] NEW ENGLAND. Andre Thevet in 1556 says Cabot purposed going to Peru and America to establish there a New England.

[8] PRINCE CHARLES, afterwards Charles I.

[9] MASSACHUSETTS first mentioned.

[10] CAPE ELIZABETH. The southern headland of Casco Bay, Me.

[11] CAPE ANN, named for the queen of James I.

[12] CHARLES RIVER, named for Prince Charles, afterwards Charles I.

[13] MERRIMACK. The Indians told Smith of this river, but he did not explore it.

INTERLUDE.—THE DOOM OF THE RED MEN.

THE reported severity of a New England winter could not make Sir Ferdinando Gorges forego his fixed purpose of establishing a colony on our shores. In order to show how groundless were the stories spread abroad by Gilbert's men he sent his agent Richard Vines [1] to pass the winter of 1616—17 at the mouth of the Saco. Vines did this.

This winter is most memorable for the fatal sickness[2] which raged among the Indians. Thousands died. Yet Vines and his men escaped although they slept in the same cabins with the dead and dying. Whole villages were depopulated. The tribes that had numbered a thousand warriors were reduced to hundreds and fifties. For years after, the bones of the unburied victims showed where the destroying angel had passed and ravaged the land.

This great mortality spread unchecked from Narragansett Bay to the Merrimack and from the Merrimack to the Penobscot. The Indians never recovered from it. It had been foretold them and they believed it was sent upon them by their Great Evil Spirit as a warning that the pale-faces should possess their land. The whites also believed that it had been sent to prepare the way for their coming. One writer of the time says that "the wondrous wisdom and love of God" was shown in sending "his minister to sweep away by heaps the savages."

When it was foretold them by their medicine-men the Indians had scornfully answered that the Manitou could not kill them all.

---

[1] RICHARD VINES is considered the pioneer settler of Maine.

[2] FATAL SICKNESS, or Great Plague, as it is usually called. Whether it was yellow-fever, small-pox, or some unknown epidemic, is equally in doubt. But it is known that small-pox periodically scourged the native tribes.

THE GREAT CHARTER OF NEW ENGLAND.

"The strongest nation is that which counts the most robust men interested in its defence, animated by its spirit, and possessing the feeling of its destiny."

WE should remember that the old Charter of Virginia had been divided between two companies. Gorges and his associates were dissatisfied with their charter because its privileges came short of what they desired. Therefore, the more effectually to put themselves on an equal footing with the South Virginia Company they asked the king to give them a new charter. Among other things they asked that their territory might be called New England. King James granted it to them. This grant is known as the Great Charter of New England,[1] it being the first on which the name of New England appears, and the one from which all subsequent grants were derived.

Man proposes, but God disposes. We shall now see how a handful of poor people, knit together in a common bond of brotherhood, did at last what the greatest lords, with the most ample means, had been unable to accomplish.

[1] GREAT CHARTER OF NEW ENGLAND, granted in 1620, extended from the fortieth to the forty-eighth parallel of north latitude, or from Philadelphia to St. Johns, Newfoundland; and from sea to sea.

II.

COMING TO STAY.

THE ARK OF NEW ENGLAND, 1620.

*"Our fathers crossed the ocean's wave
To seek this shore."—Percival.*

FOR many years the Church of England had sternly persecuted those Protestants who disobeyed its ordinances or who wished to worship God independently of its forms and ceremonies. Their preachers were imprisoned, their meetings broken up, their sanctuaries violated. Those who wished simply to reform the mother church without leaving it were reproachfully called Puritans.[1] Those who wanted nothing at all to do with it were called Separatists.

THE MAYFLOWER.

Driven by this persecution to seek an asylum in some foreign land, a congregation of these people fled with their pastor into Holland, where they could be free to worship God as they pleased.

They took up their residence in the fair city of Leyden. The Hollanders gave them a kind welcome, but the exiles felt that they were strangers in a strange land. This happened in the year 1607.

Here they dwelt in peace and love for twelve years, though struggling hard with poverty all the while. But in twelve years those who had left England in the prime of life were getting to be old men and women. In that time their sons had grown to manhood and their daughters to womanhood. The young men had grown tired of a life of hardship and restraint, and on coming of age they were leaving their parents, one by one, to seek their fortunes in the army or on the sea.

Should this go on of course it was only a question of time when the community would die out. So the exiles knowing this, began seriously to consider how to prevent it, for they hoped to increase, not diminish, to draw other Christians to them, not see themselves dwindling away by the loss of the flower of their little flock. But how should this be done?

They talked all this over, quietly and wisely, around their firesides. They discussed it long and earnestly. After much anxious thought about it they decided at last to seek another home in a distant land.

Where should they go? Some wanted to go to Guiana, some to Virginia, and others took counsel of their Dutch friends who urged the exiles to go to the new country discovered by Hendrik Hudson. And it seems this was what they really wished to do. Having decided that they would go to some part of Virginia they sought, and with much trouble finally obtained, through friends in England, a patent giving them permission to settle within the Southern Company's limits.

Here are some of the reasons they gave to show those friends why they believed they would succeed where so many had failed:—

"We are well weaned from the delicate milk of our mother country and inured to the difficulties of a strange and hard land, which yet in a great part we have by patience overcome.

"The people are, for the body of them, industrious and frugal as any company of people in the world.

"We are knit together in a most strict and sacred bond and covenant of the Lord, of the violation whereof we make great conscience, and by virtue whereof we do hold ourselves straitly tied to all care of each other's good, and of the whole by every one and so mutually.

"Lastly it is not with us as with other men whom small things can discourage or small discontentments cause to wish themselves at home again."

The men who were most forward in planning and carrying out the removal were Rev. John Robinson, the pastor, Elder William Brewster, Robert Cushman and John Carver.

These exiles were afraid of being persecuted for their religion even in Virginia. They could get no pledge from the king of freedom of worship. He would only consent to let them go unnoticed. With this promise they decided to go on, and for once the promise of a king did not fail them, for King James kept his word.

Being people of small means they procured money on very hard terms of certain London merchants, or adventurers,[2] with whom they formed a partnership. With this money they purchased the Speedwell, of forty tons, and hired the Mayflower of one hundred and eighty tons. The Speedwell came to Delft Haven[3] to take the exiles on board. Not half of the whole number went, as the more aged and infirm were left behind, but this first party was to be the pioneer company.

Those who were to stay in Holland came to bid their friends farewell. It was a sad parting. With tears

TWO PILGRIMS.

streaming down his aged cheeks their beloved pastor knelt down and earnestly prayed as his people went on board the ship that was to take them sway. He was to keep his charge over those left in Holland, while Brewster took under his care the exiles, or Pilgrims,[4] as they now called themselves.

A fair wind soon brought the Speedwell to Southampton where the Mayflower, with other emigrants, was waiting for her. On the 5th of August 1620 the two ships put to sea.

Shortly after sailing the Speedwell sprung a leak and both ships had to put back to Plymouth. This mishap discouraged many of the colonists from going on. The Speedwell proving unseaworthy the Mayflower on the 6th of September sailed alone with a hundred and two passengers on board.

---

[1] PURITANS objected to the vestments of the clergy, to making the sign of the cross, kneeling at the Communion or marrying with a ring, as "Popish" ceremonies: also to the hierarchy of the Anglican Church. They were also called Nonconformists.

[2] ADVENTURERS meant those who risked money or goods in the venture.

[3] DELFT HAVEN was celebrated for its earthenware called Delft.

[4] PILGRIM; a traveller, especially one who goes to a holy place.

EXPLORING THE WILDERNESS.

"The breaking waves dashed high
On a stern and rock-bound coast."—Hemans.

AFTER a long and stormy ocean voyage the Mayflower came in sight of Cape Cod on the 9th of November. The Pilgrims now consulted together about their destination, for they had not yet settled where it should be.

At length it was decided to find some place near Hudson River. Accordingly the ship was steered to the south, but she soon ran among the roaring breakers of Monomoy where she narrowly escaped shipwreck. Not unwillingly, it is said, the master then put back into the little harbor round the Cape, where Provincetown now crowds among the drifted sand-hills, and at last, on the 11th of November, the storm-tossed Mayflower rode safe within the harbor.

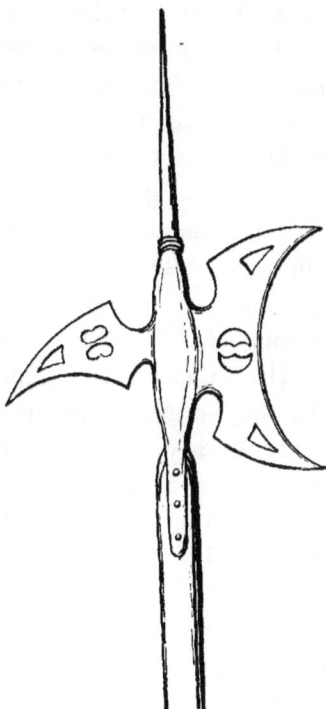

PILGRIM HALBERD.

Eagerly the weary Pilgrims scanned the inhospitable shores. Whichever way they looked they saw nothing but a wilderness of barren sand-hills which the gales of centuries had heaped up. Possibly they may have seen here and there a few lonely pines or scrubby cedars which heightened the sense of desolation, and their first feeling must have been one of bitter disappointment. No human habitation was in sight. All was as silent as at the Creation. Recollecting why this was named Cape Cod the sailors threw over their hooks, but the cod that Gosnold's men had found so plentiful could not be taken. The fishing season was past. They seemed too late for every thing.

Before going on shore the Pilgrims drew up a compact[1] by which they agreed to be governed. They did it to silence disputes and misunderstandings, which already began to trouble them, and to establish necessary rules for the good of all, otherwise they would have been living without law, or as outlaws. So they signed this compact in the Mayflower's cabin. No simpler form of government was ever devised. In a few terse sentences it embodied the whole philosophy of government.

The Pilgrims; amply proved its sufficiency, for it was the only organic law they ever had. It therefore stands alone in history as the first act of self-government by the people of New England. The Pilgrims were now a body politic[2] of their own creation and they had thus originated the first Commonwealth[3] of the New World.

They also chose John Carver[4] to be their governor. Before this they had no civil officers, or any bond to hold them together except that of fellowship in the church. So these two important acts being done they were now ready to begin their settlement as soon as a suitable place could be found. Winter was close at hand so they must do what they would do quickly.

So while the Mayflower lay quietly at anchor under the shelter of Long Point[5] three exploring parties were sent to search for a proper site to settle upon.

In the first place they must find a good harbor—that is one with deep water, a secure anchorage, well protected and easy of access. Fishery was to be their chief employment, therefore they must not be located too far from the open sea for boats to go and return quickly. To these general requirements were added those of soil fit for tillage, timber for building, wood for fuel and good water—running water, to do away with the need for digging wells. Then the general situation in respect to health and for defence was also to be considered.

In the second place it should be remembered that the Pilgrims had not meant to settle in New England at all, but were in a measure driven to do so by the lateness of the season and the refusal or

INDIAN SAGAMORE'S GRAVE.

inability of their shipmaster to take them farther south. Therefore, while the previous explorations of this coast must have been known to them in a general way, it is clear that they had not been studied with an eye to any practical use.

By making their task much more difficult, these wants and these drawbacks rendered its success all the more creditable.

The first party went as far as Pa´met River.[6] The second went as far as Wellfleet harbor. They saw

Indians who ran away from them, and they found wigwams abandoned by their owners, and cornfields and
Indian graves [7] in various places, but they saw nothing
to their liking for a place of abode and so returned dis-
appointed to the ship.

At one place they discovered what they took for graves.
Curiosity led them to dig there, when, to their great wonder, they found Indian corn buried in the ground. Some
of this was taken for seed, but in order to get it they
had to hew and hack the frozen ground with their
swords.

These burrows were the Indian barns or granaries.
A hole was first dug. This was lined at the bottom and
sides with rush mats. Then baskets containing the ears
of yellow, red, and blue-speckled corn were put in and
the whole covered with earth. Some of these mounds
would hold a hogshead of corn. Farmers in the
country even now keep potatoes over winter in this
way, and silos are but a modern adaptation of the
idea.

This store of corn was a goodly sight to the explorers, for they had before seen nothing of the kind, nor
did they know where to get it. In another place they
found the grave of a European whom they supposed to
have fallen into the hands of the savages, and perished
among them, also sundry articles of European make,
as well as Indian bowls, trays, platters, baskets and
earthen pots.

While these parties were out, the people in the ship
went freely on shore, the men to gather firewood and
fetch water, the women to wash their clothing and
refresh themselves after their long confinement on shipboard.

[1] COMPACT, printed in full in "Nooks and Corners of the New England Coast," p. 267.

[2] BODY POLITIC, citizens assuming the powers and responsibilities of government.

[3] COMMONWEALTH, a free State.

[4] JOHN CARVER brought his wife Katherine, Desire Minter and two men-servants with him, but no children. Carver, Mass., is named for him.

[5] LONG POINT is the extreme point of Cape Cod harbor.

[6] PAMET RIVER (Indian) nearly divides Truro in two.

[7] INDIAN GRAVES. The Indians here placed their dead in the ground. In other parts of the country they were placed on scaffolds or suspended among the branches of the trees, as a protection against wild beasts.

THE FIRST ENCOUNTER.

"Mery it was in grene forest
Among the leves grene,
When that men walke east and west
With bowes and arrowes kene."—Old Ballad.

NEARLY a whole month had been uselessly spent in searching the shores of Cape Cod. The bleak December had now come in with its frost and snow, its icy blasts, its short days and long weary nights.

Eighteen picked men, every man with his musket, his sword and his corselet, now pushed off in the shallop in order if possible to end the suspense. Four of the eighteen were the most valiant and prudent men among the Pilgrims.[1] All had volunteered for this expedition. A part landed and made a painful march through the swamps and thickets of Eastham, while the shallop coasted along the shore in company.

Overtaken by night the tired and hungry explorers hastily threw up a brushwood shelter, built a fire, set a watch, and bivouacked on the frozen ground.

They were roused by a hideous outcry in the middle of the night. "Arm! arm!" cried their sentinel. Seizing their arms the whites fired one or two random shots in the darkness when the noises ceased. Thinking it must have been wolves howling round the camp, the Pilgrims again threw themselves upon the ground.

They were early astir, getting ready for another journey. Some shot off their wet pieces, others carried their arms and armor down to the beach, meaning to put them on board the shallop when the tide was high enough to let her come in to the shallow shore.

While mostly disarmed, and eating their breakfast around their fire in the dusk of the morning, without fear, again their sentinel suddenly ran in among them shouting "Indians! Indians!" At the same time Indian yells broke out on all sides of them.[2]

FORDING A RIVER.

Those who had left their arms on the beach now ran to recover them before they should be intercepted by the foe. As they did so the arrows flew thick and fast. The Indians shot fiercely and vengefully. With savage yells they charged close up to the camp where only four of the Pilgrims stood on their defence. These however stood firm and returned the fire as soon as they could. Still, the Pilgrims were hard pushed, for their friends in the shallop were unable to come to their rescue until one brave fellow waded off to them with a firebrand, from the shore. Then both parties opened a scattered fire. But the first advantage was with the assailants.

After a short, sharp fight the Indians were driven into the woods which they filled with dismal howlings.

The English then went on board their shallop to go to another place along the coast which their pilot had told them was a good harbor. No one had been hurt in this first encounter. But their escape made the Pilgrims more prudent and cautious as well as acquainted them with the wily ways of the savages.

While sailing for this harbor a storm of snow and sleet came up. They crowded sail until the shallop's mast snapped in the gale and the rudder became unshipped. With mast and rudder gone the men strove heroically to keep the boat afloat, but at every moment the big waves swept over them and they were being steadily driven toward the breakers.[3] The pilot cried out in

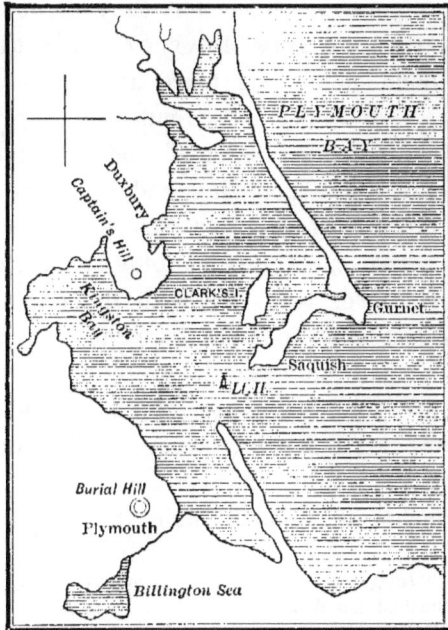

PLYMOUTH BAY AND HARBOR.

fear, as they neared the shore, that he had never seen the place before. All at once, when they were almost in the surf, the sailor who held the steering oar cried out, "Row for your lives!" By great exertions they pushed into a safer anchorage. Wet to the skin, and numb with cold, they reached the shore, built a fire, and waited for the morning. When daylight came they

found they were on an island.[4]   Giving thanks to God
for their escape both from the savages and the sea they
passed that day in exploring the island, and the next
being the Sabbath they rested.

On Monday they sounded the harbor and made an
excursion into the land. The harbor they had been so
providentially driven into by stress of weather seemed
so good to them that they hastened back to the ship
with the glad news of their discovery. They had
found an abiding place at last!

Two important events had happened while the ship
lay in harbor at Cape Cod. A child had been born and
one of the company had been drowned. The child was
the son of William White and was called Peregrine;
the passenger was Dorothy, the beloved wife of William
Bradford, who was with the exploring party when this
distressing accident happened.

Again the Mayflower hoisted sail and ploughed out
into the bay. Soon the high headland of the island
appeared in sight and on the 16th day of December
they joyfully entered the harbor of Plymouth and cast
anchor that should hold the world.

---

[1] THESE FOUR were Carver, Standish, Bradford and Winslow.

[2] THESE ADVERSARIES were Nauset Indians, a very fierce and warlike tribe inhabiting Cape Cod. The same who had attacked De Monts' men.

[3] BREAKERS of Sa'quish head; northeast point of Plymouth Bay. Saquish is Indian for clams.

[4] CLARK'S ISLAND, named for the master's-mate of the Mayflower, who was one of the party. There is here a large bowlder with the inscription, taken from Mourt's "Relation," "On the Sabboth Day wee rested."

THE LANDING OF THE PILGRIM FATHERS IN NEW ENGLAND.

HEMANS.

THE breaking waves dashed high
   On a stern and rock-bound coast,
And the woods against a stormy sky
   Their giant branches tossed;

And the heavy night hung dark
   The hills and waters o'er,
When a band of exiles moored their bark
   On the wild New England shore.

Not as the conqueror comes,
   They the true-hearted came;
Not with the roll of the stirring drums,
   And the trumpet that sings of fame:

Not as the flying come,
   In silence and in fear;—
They shook the depths of the desert gloom
   With their hymns of lofty cheer.

Amidst the storm they sang,
   And the stars heard and the sea;
And the sounding aisles of the dim woods rang
   To the anthem of the free!

The ocean-eagle soared
   From his nest by the white wave's foam;
And the rocking pines of the forest roared—
   This was their welcome home!

There were men with hoary hair
   Amidst that pilgrim band;—
Why had they come to wither there,
   Away from their childhood's land?

There was woman's fearless eye,
  Lit by her deep love's truth;
There was manhood's brow serenely high,
  And the fiery heart of youth.

what sought they thus afar?
  Bright jewels of the mine?
The wealth of seas, the spoils of war?—
  They sought a faith's pure shrine!

Ay, call it holy ground,
  The soil where first they trod!
They have left unstain'd what there they found—
  Freedom to worship God.

ON PLYMOUTH ROCK.

"The trappings of a monarchy will set up a Commonwealth."—Milton.

BY a strange chance Captain Smith, or rather Prince Charles, his patron, had given the name of Plymouth to this very place. Should we not pause in wonder at these singular events in history? And can we help feeling a guiding Hand was with them?

After making further examination of the harbor and the shore which bad weather very much retarded, the Pilgrims finally made choice of a hillside sloping gently down from its summit to the bay.[1]

LANDING OF THE PILGRIMS.

They chose it principally because a large tract of land had already been cleared by the Indians at this place and lay ready to their hand to plant or build upon.

The hard work of clearing a site was therefore saved them which was a matter of grave consequence at this time of year. On one side was a running brook[2] which they found to be excellent water. Good timber trees for building were rather far off, yet even this was better than having the forest too near, for since their fight with

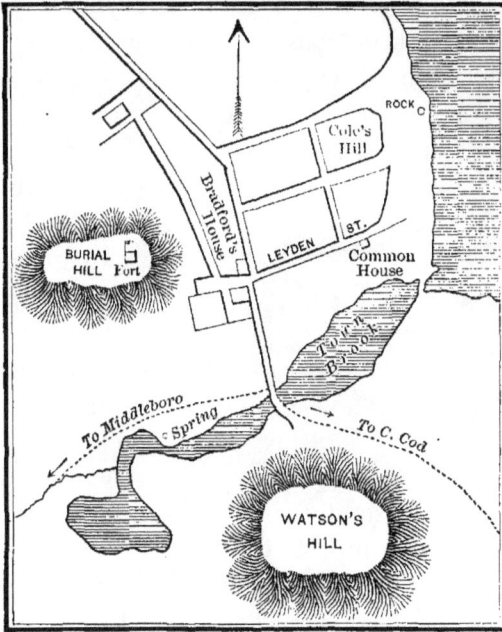

LANDMARKS OF PLYMOUTH.

the Indians the Pilgrims felt that their chief safety lay in their weapons, and it was better to have the woods, in which they lurked to steal slyly upon them, as far off as possible.

Then the hill was another important advantage to them because from its top approaching ships could be espied far out to sea, while upon land the presence of enemies might seasonably be detected. Here they could fix their lookout and plant their cannon to command the town and anchorage.

This decision was not reached until the 20th of December. On that night twenty men encamped on the site that had been chosen. The next day the shallop brought them provisions from the ship. They made this their rendezvous and kept constant watch over it.[3] From that memorable 20th of December 1620, the founding of Plymouth should be reckoned, for from that day the ground they stood upon has never ceased to be trodden by the white men. What they held was never abandoned; and from that moment the colony with varying fortunes continued to increase till it overspread the land.

Tradition has kept the memory of the rock on which the Pilgrims first set foot, and which lay on the strand at the foot of the hill. It has become an historic spot, to which the name Forefathers' Rock[4] has been given. No other in America possesses such hallowed associations or has so often been celebrated in song and story.

"Here," says De Tocqueville, "is a stone which the feet of a few outcasts pressed for an instant, and the stone becomes famous. It is treasured by a nation. Its very dust is shared as a relic. And what has become of the gateways of a thousand palaces? Who cares for them?"

Tradition also gives to two persons the credit of having first leaped upon the rock. Mary Chilton the Pilgrim maiden and young John Alden are the ones for whom this honor is claimed, as we read in the lines to Mary Chilton,

> "The first on Plymouth Rock to leap!
>   Among the timid flock she stood,
>   Rare figure, near the Mayflower's prow,
>   With heart of Christian fortitude,
>   And light heroic on her brow!"

But if we do not certainly know who is entitled to this honor we do know that the act is cherished as the first step toward founding a nation, and as typical of the heroism and daring of its founders. And such it will stand for all time as one of the grand stepping-stones of history.

We know, moreover, that from the day of their first landing, the Pilgrims were constantly passing between the ship and the shore until dwellings could be erected to shelter them. As many of the women went on shore at Cape Cod it is reasonable to suppose that they went on shore here; and it would be just like a romping lass to jump into the boat and strive to be first to land, when the final determination was made.

On every fine day the work went on as expeditiously as mid-winter weather would permit. Working-parties came off from the ship to assist those who staid on shore. Some went into the woods to fell trees, some carried timber, some sawed, some used beetle and wedge and some plied the mattock or spade. All worked with a will, nor were any excused from labor except the weak or sickly.

We may imagine these Pilgrims standing ankle-deep in snow while wielding the adze or broad-axe with be-numbed hands, yet tenderly glancing now and again across the still bay to where their wives and little ones were watching them from the Mayflower's deck and thinking on the homes their husbands or fathers were rearing for them, with their strong arms and stout hearts, in that lonely place.

On Christmas Day they began building their magazine. [5] Toward night the Indians gave them an alarm. The men dropped their tools and seized their muskets but soon all was quiet again.

In a few days things were so far in readiness that a party was set to work on the hill where it was meant to plant their cannon. At this time the ground was measured off for the houses, and for greater convenience also, the whole number of

MEMORIAL OVER FOREFATHERS' ROCK.

people were formed into nineteen families, all single men being required to join some family. This was done that there might be fewer houses to build, as well as less ground to inclose, as was necessary to their safety. Each head of a family cast lots for his homestead. When he had chosen it the ground was staked out upon which he should build. Every family had enough land for a garden-plot, larger or smaller according to the number of the household.

It was agreed that each man should build his own house. But the common-house, or rendezvous, was the first to be built. All were of one pattern. Rough-hewn logs were hauled by hand to the spot. Tenons were cut at the ends and the logs were then laid one upon another. This made four strong walls. Over this the roof timbers were roughly framed and fitted, and then covered in with bundles of flags or bulrushes, cut in the swamps and called thatch. Chimneys and fireplaces probably would be built of stone. Lastly the crevices between the logs, and the chinks in the chimney, were plastered with mud-mortar mixed with straw, inside and out.

This made a solid building, but though excellent for shedding the rain the thatch would easily take fire.

In fact, early one morning, while the rendezvous was as full of men as could lie in it, all of them having their muskets loaded by their sides, a spark set the thatch on fire. Governor Carver and William Bradford were lying sick in the house at the time and were in great danger of being blown up before they could be got out, as the colonists had their store of powder in the house. Little damage was done however, as only the thatch burnt, leaving the frame uninjured.

The Pilgrims built only seven dwellings during the first winter. Next to the rendezvous, and a shed to put their stores in, one of their first needs was a hospital —and this was soon built, and soon filled with the sick, for exposure to wet and cold, poor fare and worse lodg-ing, soon told on even the most rugged frames. Hardly a day went by without a death followed by a hurried burial. On some days two or three died. At one time not more than six or seven were left in sound health to care for the rest. So we see the sad experience of De Monts' colony repeated at Plymouth; and we also see why no more houses were built.

While this sore distress lay so heavily upon them the Pilgrims dared not send away their ship. Indeed, the Mayflower herself became a floating hospital, disease having infected the ship's company as well as the colonists.

When spring came nearly half the original colonists were dead. One by one their sorrowing friends had laid them under the cold sod of Cole's Hill,[6] near by the shore, but for fear that the Indians might discover their losses, and seek to overpower them in their weakness, even the graves were levelled.

With warmer weather the disease began to abate, but for many a year the stoutest men showed its effects on the system in their enfeebled frames. "Our arms and legs tell us to this day," are the words of one describing their condition, "what we have suffered." Fifty odd half-starved, emaciated men and women were all that this terrible winter had spared.

In his "Pilgrim's Vision," the poet Holmes portrays with mingled pathos and humor the cabin-home of a primitive settler:

> "His home was a freezing cabin
>   Too bare for the hungry rat;
>   Its roof was thatched with ragged grass,
>   And bald enough of that.
>   The hole that served for a casement
>   Was glazed with an ancient hat;
>   And the ice was gently thawing
>   From the log whereon he sat."

In April the Mayflower sailed for England. She carried sad news to those who were anxiously waiting for tidings of the Pilgrims.

To this village in the wilderness the Pilgrims gave the name of New Plymouth, thus distinguishing it from Old Plymouth, the port from which they had last sailed in England. For they were Englishmen and loved their country still.

"With toil and fatigue, perhaps not to be conceived by their brethren and fellow subjects at home, and with the constant fear of their lives from a numerous, savage, and warlike race of men, they began the settlement and God prospered them."

[1] BURIAL HILL, so-called from being used as a place of interment. *See* Cole's Hill.

[2] TOWN BROOK rising in Billington Sea. The bank of the stream was probably the public washing-ground for the women who used a battledore to beat the clothes with.

[3] THEY PROBABLY built a brushwood shelter as they had done before, afterward using tents or spare sails from the ship, temporarily.

[4] FOREFATHERS' ROCK lies at the foot of Cole's Hill which rises abruptly above the shore. A memorial canopy has been built over it, in which are deposited the remains of many who were buried on this hill, the first winter, and subsequently disinterred. The tradition of the rock is fully accepted. In 1769 the Old Colony Club began the formal commemoration of the 22d of December as Forefathers' Day. Some societies however observe the 21st.

[5] MAGAZINE or Common-House for storing powder, arms, tools and provisions. It stood on the south side of Leyden Street. The Pilgrims lodged in it till other houses were made ready. *See* plan.

[6] COLE'S HILL is a lower spur of Burial hill. *See* plan: also note 4.

LIFE IN THE OLD COLONY.

"In good Old Colony times
When we lived under the King."—Old Song.

AS soon as a house was ready a family moved into it with their household goods. The next thing was to set the house in order.

The better sort of furniture showed certain household distinctions which were strictly observed. High-backed, broad-bottomed, roomy arm-chairs were for grown up people only. And hence gran'ther's, or father's or mother's chair became a household word. The youth or servants had wooden settles,[1] or benches, or stools to sit on. The little ones had crickets. In the chamber were high-posted bedsteads, on which hung the Pilgrim's night-cap, with truckle-beds for children of tender age. The babies slept in odd little cradles, like that shown in the engraving.

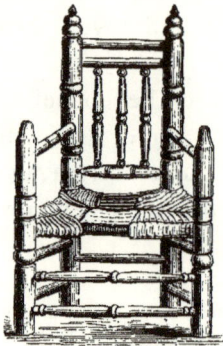

GOV. CARVER'S CHAIR.

Perhaps a braided mat or rug may have helped to cover the bare floor, but there was no such thing as a carpet in the house, and seldom a picture. Yet we think loving hands must soon have made even the rudest cabin look tidy and homelike.

One small room had to serve nearly every domestic purpose. This room contained the big fireplace in which all the cooking was done. It also contained the oaken table at which the family sat down to their daily meals.

In one corner a few shelves held the family dishes. This was called the dresser, and may sometimes be seen in old country houses now. Pewter and iron were the metals for service. Rows of pewter plates, platters, and

FULLER CRADLE.

tankards, porringers, and candlesticks, ewers and basins, all bright with daily scouring, shone from these shelves and lighted up the room.[2] Some platters were four or

five spans broad. Possibly a little Holland-delft or a few silver spoons, or a silver porringer, the gift of some fond godmother, may have been found in some houses, but not as a rule. The other corners would be naturally occupied by the family spinning-wheel, and by the

KITCHEN FIREPLACE.

arms belonging to the head of the house—his corselet, morion, sword, and trusty matchlock, with rest and bandoleer. For a while shift was made with oiled paper instead of glass for windows; and a notch cut on the frame told the hour of noon, and was called a noonmark.

Before friction matches were invented, lighting a fire was no very simple matter as it is now. The Pilgrim had to get down on his knees, as he often did, to strike fire with flint and steel among a handful of dry tinder-stuff; consequently great care was taken not to let the fire go out. The embers were always carefully covered at night. This very old custom long kept alive the term "curfew"[3] as signalling the hour for extinguishing fires and going to bed.

As no one sat up late lamps were little used. The pitch-pine knot obtained its name of candlewood from being used as a substitute for oil or tallow.

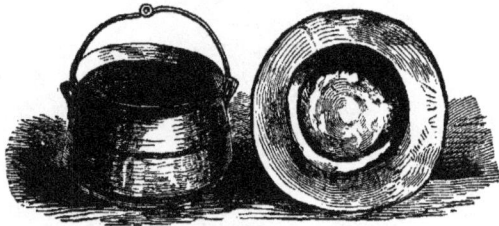

IRON POT AND PEWTER PLATTER.

Meat was roasted on iron spits [4] which had to be kept constantly turning to prevent the meat from burning or roasting on one side. Iron kettles, hung on a bit of chain, were used for boiling. Bread was baked in Dutch ovens or skillets set on a bed of coals, raked over the hearth; and red-herring were roasted in hot ashes in the same way.

A coarse kind of bread, made of wheat, rye, or barley meal, and eaten with a draught of spring water was the daily diet. Each family's weekly allowance of bread or meal was carefully served out to it. The Pilgrims had also some supply of ship-bread, butter, English pease and salted meat. But it was only when some lucky hunter brought in a deer that they could have fresh meat, though sometimes a wild fowl and now and then a stray fish found its way to the Pilgrim's table. Usually they had just enough to keep famine from their doors. This was the way they lived the first winter.

"With sometimes fish and sometimes fast,
That household store may longer last."

By and by, after the settlers had raised their first crop of corn, the Indians taught them how to prepare it for food. The kernels were first pounded in a mortar and the meal sifted. What went through the sieve was called *samp,* the coarse remainder hominy. The samp was used instead of flour, and the whites learned to make bread of it. The hominy was put in an iron pot, water added, and the whole boiled over a gentle fire to the thickness

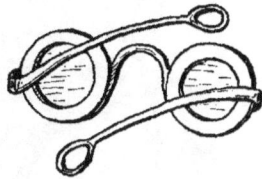

SPECTACLES.

of pudding. When eaten with milk this was found to be a very wholesome dish and for a long time it was the standing New England article of food.

The Indians also gathered quantities of the sort of huckleberry, called bilberry, which they dried and sold to the English, who used them for puddings instead of currants. Cranberries were also gathered for winter use. The Pilgrims found them an excellent antidote for scurvy. Cape Cod is now noted for its valuable and extensive cranberry meadows.

These things somewhat enlarged the Pilgrims' meagre diet. Of course the summer was a season of plenty, as they could then get lobsters and clams and other kinds of fish. But in winter none of these were to be had.

The Indians also taught the English the names and uses of many simple indigenous roots and herbs. They already knew of the medicinal properties of sassafras bark, and sarsaparilla root, both of which grew wild in the Plymouth woods.

The clothing worn by the Pilgrims was made from such coarse woollen stuffs as best suited their employ-

FLAX SPINNING-WHEEL.

ments and condition, for though some were masters and some servants, a common necessity made all fare alike in the drudgery of outdoor or indoor labor. Both men and women wore high-crowned felt hats "perked up like the shaft of a temple," but hoods or kerchiefs were the common head-wear of the women when they went abroad.

A doublet or tunic of some dark color, confined at the waist by a belt, loose trunks or trousers, reaching to the knee and tied, woollen stockings coming up to the knee, with stout shoes, was the usual attire of the men; and frequently a short cloak was worn out of doors by both sexes. This made a garb at once sensible and picturesque.

All the women could spin and most of them knew how to weave cloth. Some could embroider prettily and some had learned the arts of dyeing and lace-making in Holland. Most were equally expert with needle or distaff.

For several years the Pilgrims had no domestic animals except one or two dogs. In 1624, Edward Winslow brought over one bull and three heifers. Goats and swine were introduced at a later day than the time of our narrative.

Poverty taught the Pilgrims economy, necessity taught them to be industrious, hardship inculcated its lessons of patience, fortitude and trust in God and one another.

[1] SETTLES were wooden benches with high backs; usually long enough for three or four persons.

[2] OTHER ARTICLES of domestic use were wooden platters (trenchers), trays, piggins, bowls and bottles. Glass in any form was not common. Iron pots and pot-hooks, fire-shovels, tongs, and-irons, and bellows were in common use. Many articles used by the Pilgrims may be seen in Pilgrim Hall, Plymouth.

[3] CURFEW, from *couvre-feu*. Introduced by the Normans into England and enforced by royal edict.

[4] SPITS were iron prongs on which the joint was hung or skewered. A more primitive way was to suspend it by a string from a stick laid across two upright ones.

LIFE IN THE OLD COLONY—*Continued.*

For a long time the Indians kept away from the settlement. Now and then they could be seen lurking about in the edge of the woods, but slunk away when any one tried to approach them. They certainly were not friendly, and could not be trusted, and the Pilgrims wisely resolved to be prepared for them should they make an attack. So a company was formed and Myles Standish[1] chosen its captain.

'Short of stature he was, but strongly built and athletic,
Broad in the shoulders, deep-chested, with muscles and sinews of
    iron."

The Mayflower's sailors helped them drag their great guns to the top of the hill where they were kept ready for service.

In the middle of March, while the men were at work as usual, an Indian came boldly into the village. He was nearly naked and came all alone. He walked straight on through the rows of houses until he reached the rendezvous which he was about to enter when the settlers stopped him. Before they could get over their surprise this stranger savage said to them in good English, "Welcome Englishmen!"

They threw a cloak over his shoulders and gave him some bread and meat.

He told them he was Samoset and a sagamore[2] in his own country, which was a day's sail from theirs with a great wind. By questioning him they found out that he had learned to speak English from the fishermen who came to Monhegan every year.

STANDISH'S SWORD.

Samoset also told them that the place they were in was called Patuxet by his people. The Indians, he said, had all died at the time of the plague, so that none were left to dispute the right of the English to dwell there. This news quieted the fears of the Pilgrims. They also learned that soon after their arrival the surviving Indians of those parts had met together in a dark swamp, where, after solemnly cursing the pale-faces, their conjurors had called on the Evil Spirit to destroy them.

He also told them why their red neighbors were so unfriendly toward them. It was, he said, all owing to

Captain Hunt's having treacherously carried off so many of their friends from this very place. They thought all Englishmen must be equally treacherous.

Many other things Samoset told them which they were glad to know. The Pilgrims made out to understand his broken English but he promised shortly to bring another Indian, named Squanto, who talked much better than he could.

This friendly native, coming thus unawares among them, proved a true and faithful ally. He acted as mediator between the Pilgrims and the neighboring tribes. He carried offers of friendship to the great chief Massasoit,³ which presently ripened into a lasting peace, so that instead of living in daily fear of their lives the Pilgrims wrote home that they walked the wild woods as peaceably and safely as their friends did the highways of Old England.

Very soon Squanto came to Plymouth. He was the only one left of all the Indians who had lived there, for Captain Hunt had kidnapped him and so saved his life. The Pilgrims adopted Squanto and he lived with them as one of their community until he died.

Squanto became useful in many ways. He told the settlers when and how to plant their corn as the Indians did, to plant when the oak leaf was as big as the mouse's ear and to drop one or two herrings in each hill if they would have a good yield. Squanto hunted and fished for them. Squanto was their trusty guide, interpreter and messenger. Squanto held the Indians in awe by telling them that the white men kept the plague buried in the ground and could let it loose among the Indians whenever they pleased.

In the first planting-time Governor Carver was taken

sick while at work in the field and died after a very
short illness. The Pilgrims wanted to show him all the
respect they could, for he was much beloved. Having
neither hearse nor funeral trappings, the soldiers bore
the body to the grave, and fired volleys over this brave
and true man's last resting place. They then chose
William Bradford to be their governor in Carver's
place.

We find evidence of few vices among the Pilgrims.
They were a too deeply religious folk for that. Some-

RELICS OF THE PILGRIMS.

what austere they certainly were yet kindly in all their
relations with each other. The Golden Rule seems to
have been the practice of their lives. No doubt they
had acquired something of the national phlegm and
steadiness of the Dutch character but not the habit of
excessive drinking which characterized the Hollanders
of that time.

Amusements were even fewer. Dancing was considered an unseemly practice. Stage-plays were thought
to be the device of the Evil One. Indulgence in out-

of-door sports was looked upon as a foolish, if not sinful, waste of time. Yet the singing of psalms, or perhaps some of the exquisite madrigals of the day, no doubt often sweetened the hours of relaxation from daily toil.

Morning and evening prayers were never omitted. For whether the Pilgrim had only a crust or cup of water made no difference to him in the matter of giving thanks. And he always found something to be thankful for.

Like all people of their time the Pilgrims believed in signs and portents, phantoms and witches, and in other supernatural appearances. Great or unusual storms, comets or earthquakes, were thought to be the sure forerunners of some calamity.

The Pilgrims did not observe Christmas or Easter or any of the festival days of the Church of England— only the Christian Sabbath and such days as were set apart for fasting or thanksgiving were kept as holy days. [5]

It was the custom for the governor to call all the able-bodied men together every day and lead them to their work in the field or elsewhere. On Christmas day they were called as usual, but some who were newly come there said that it was against their consciences to work on that day. The governor told them that in that case he would excuse them. He then led away the rest. When those who had worked came home at noon they found the conscientious ones playing at stool-ball,[6] and casting the bar,[7] in the street. The governor went to them and took away their implements. He told them it was against his conscience that they should play while others worked. If they made keeping the day a matter of devotion they must stay in their houses; but there must be no gaming or revelling in the streets.

Marriage was considered a civil contract and was performed as in Holland, by a magistrate. No Pilgrim maiden would have consented to be wedded with a ring for the world, as that was thought to be a Romish custom. Edward Winslow [8] and Susannah Whitewere the first couple married at Plymouth.

HER WEDDING-SLIPPER.

The Pilgrims showed much discretion and no little invention in inflicting punishments. Two young serving-men having quarrelled proceeded to fight it out with sword and dagger. Both men were wounded. The Pilgrims abhorred duelling. So these young men were sentenced to be tied hand and foot together, and kept without food for twenty-four hours. Another, who had tried to stir up a revolt, was marched through a double file of soldiers, every one of whom gave him a thump with the but of his musket as he passed them.

Because they had bound themselves to their merchant partners for a term of seven years the Pilgrims lived in a state of wretched servitude. All property, whether houses, lands, or goods, was held in common and was to be divided in common at the end of these seven years. No man owned a foot of land or the house he lived in. The merchants had a monopoly of the trade. They oppressed the Pilgrims with exorbitant charges for every thing sent to the colony or money lent. In six years the Pilgrims bought themselves free and from that time they began to prosper.

The Pilgrims very much desired a legal grant of the land they had settled on. They knew they were intruders. Sir F. Gorges assisted them in obtaining one, but as it did not meet their wants they procured another in 1629, which first laid down the boundaries of the colony and under which they lived until their union with Massachusetts in 1692.

One day a Narragansett Indian brought into the settlement a bundle of arrows wrapped in a snakeskin. He then hurriedly left. When Squanto saw the arrows he told the English that this meant a defiance. Though they were so few, it would not do to show any fear. So the governor stuffed the snakeskin full of powder and bullets, and then sent it back to Canonicus, chief of the Narragansetts, with the message that if he wanted war the English were ready for him whenever he chose to begin.

In four years the settlement had increased to only one hundred and eighty persons with thirty-two houses, arranged in the following manner:

One broad street, about eight hundred yards long, led up the hill from the waterside. Another crossed this at right angles, going south to the brook and north along the hillside. The houselots were all enclosed within a stout palisade which also took in the fort on the hill, so that the whole town was well protected against any sudden attack.

The ends of the streets were closed by three wooden gates, which were every night securely fastened at the setting of the watch.

In the centre, where the streets crossed, was a square enclosure on which four small guns were placed to flank the streets, thus turning the whole village into a little fortress with a central place of arms, or rallying point, from which the settlers could sweep all the streets with cannon and musketry.

At one corner of the place of arms (Town Square) stood the governor's house. Farther down the street that led to the water (Leyden Street), [9] and not far from it, was the common-house. The burial-place was outside the palisade.

Upon the hilltop the settlers had built a large, square block-house of thick planks, stayed with oak beams, with a flat roof on which were six cannon of light metal. They also built a watch-tower. These guns commanded the town and its approaches. The lower part of the block-house was used as a church, so that this building was both a castle and a house of God.

DRUMMERS AND FIFERS, 1620.

When the Sabbath came round, at the appointed hour the drummer came out into the street and beat a loud call on his drum. At this signal each family came out of its house and walked toward the rendezvous. The men were all armed as if going to battle. With matchlocks shouldered they silently fell into ranks, precisely like soldiers obeying the call to arms. Their sergeant formed them, three abreast, in front of Captain Standish's house. He then placed himself at their head.

Behind this armed escort came the governor, in a long robe. At his right hand was Elder Brewster, with his cloak on. At his left marched Standish, carrying a small cane in his hand. Next came the women leading their little ones by the hand. The servants came last. When all were in their places Standish gave the signal to march. All then took their way up the hill in this order. Upon entering their church each man put down his musket where he could instantly lay hold of it. Thus, even in the sanctuary they were on guard night and day.

As the Pilgrims made the early Christians their model their service was of the simplest kind. First Elder Brewster prayed. Then Deacon Fuller gave out a psalm, line by line, which the congregation sang. After the singing, the Elder read a lesson from Scripture and explained it. Then Bradford or some other leading man in the church spoke in meeting, or as they termed it, he "prophesied." After this the deacon put the congregation in mind of the collection to which every one gave his mite. Another psalm and another prayer ended the simple service.

Each Sabbath a constable went the round of the plantation to hunt up all who absented themselves from meeting. If they could give no good excuse they were punished.

The Pilgrims admitted none but church members to full citizenship. Those who were "on their particular," or in other words were not joined to the Pilgrim body as partners, had no voice in public affairs. A court of election was held once a year, at which time the principal officers were chosen. Then, after dispersion had broken up the primitive usage first established, as over one large family, the new settlements sent their delegates to Plymouth and a House of Representatives was formed in 1639.

In summing up the elements which made this colony
a success due weight must be given to the influence of
the family tie. The Pilgrims established for themselves
a home not in name alone, but in the fullest sense of

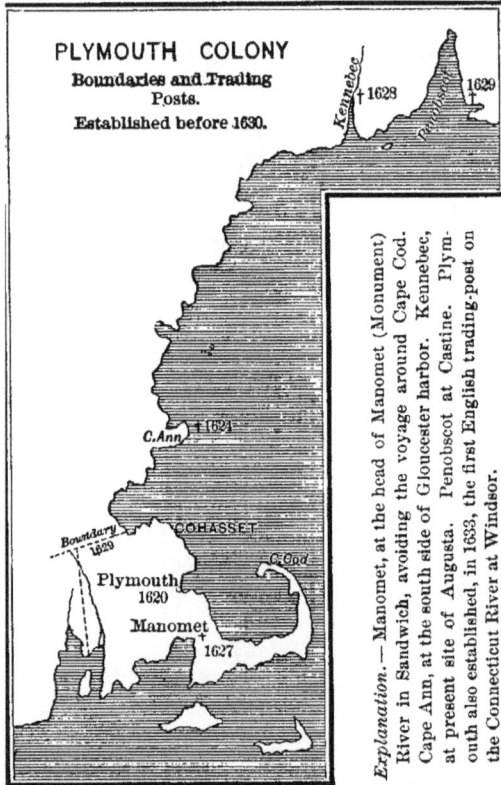

PLYMOUTH COLONY
Boundaries and Trading
Posts.
Established before 1630.

Explanation. — Manomet, at the head of Manomet (Monument)
River in Sandwich, avoiding the voyage around Cape Cod.
Cape Ann, at the south side of Gloucester harbor. Kennebec,
at present site of Augusta. Penobscot at Castine. Plymouth also established, in 1633, the first English trading-post on
the Connecticut River at Windsor.

CHART SHOWING OUTGROWTH FOR TRADE.

the word. Their wives, mothers, sisters and sweethearts
shared all their toils and privations with a fortitude
beyond praise. The Pilgrim sat at his own hearth-stone
surrounded by all that the world holds dear, and had
ever before him the highest incentive to noble deeds.

He was no castaway brooding in solitude over his hard lot. Homesickness, that stumbling-block of so many promising schemes, could not enter his humble cabin to steal away his courage. Others spoke of England as their home. The Pilgrim toiled or fought for the home his own hands had reared. His life was indeed narrow and pathetic, but woman's influence by its power to hold him steadfast wrought out the best results in that little community.

[1] MYLES STANDISH had been a soldier of fortune in the Low Countries. Little is known of him previous to his coming with the Pilgrims. He claimed descent from the Standishes of Lancashire, Eng. He cast his lot in with the Pilgrims though he did not belong to their church; and brought his wife Rose with him to Plymouth. She died the first winter. Standish afterward removed to Duxbury where Captain's Hill is named for him. *See* Longfellow's "Courtship of Miles Standish."

[2] SAMOSET belonged to the Kennebec Indians.

[3] MASSASOIT lived at Pokanoket, now Warren, R.I.

[4] WILLIAM BRADFORD fled from Austerfield, Eng., his birthplace, to Amsterdam, to escape persecution. At Amsterdam he learned the trade of silk-dyeing. With others he joined the Leyden Pilgrims when they decided to emigrate. He is admitted to have been the ablest man among them.

[5] FAST, the first was held in 1623 on account of a drought. The first general fast was Aug. 6, 1630. In 1639, the 28th of November was appointed a day of public THANKSGIVING in all the churches of Plymouth Colony.

[6] STOOL-BALL was played by any number of persons. Each player had a stool, which he set upon the ground, taking his place in front of it. The object was to throw the ball so as to hit the antagonist's stool, as in cricket, only the hands were used instead of bats.

[7] CASTING THE BAR was a trial of strength and skill.

[8] EDWARD WINSLOW came of a good English family. He joined the Leyden Church in 1617; was governor of Plymouth Colony several times, and one of its best men. Cromwell sent him on an important mission to Jamaica, in which service he died.

[9] LEYDEN STREET named for Leyden, in Holland. It runs along the south side of Cole's Hill.

III.

HISTORIC STEPPING-STONES.

FIRST COMERS IN BOSTON BAY, 1621-1626.

THE Pilgrims had heard much of the country to the north of them, called Massachusetts,[1] which Captain Smith and others had lauded as being the paradise of New England. Therefore as soon as the first spring came they sent an exploring party to it.

Squanto had told the explorers that these Massachusetts Indians were bad people who had often threatened them, and as if to prove the truth of what he said most of the Indians ran away as soon as they discovered the English.

But the Pilgrims wished to get their friendship. So they treated with all kindness those whom they met, and by and by those who had fled came back on seeing that no harm was meant them. In a little while they became so eager to trade that the Indian women would take off their beaver coats and give them for English wares.

Though subject to Massasoit, as their great head, these Massachusetts Indians had their own petty rulers or sachems who stood in the same light to Massasoit as

104

the governors of little provinces do to their king, only
the rule of each sachem over his own tribe was absolute. Indeed, the form of government among these
Indians was much the same as that existing in Europe

OPENING TRADE WITH INDIANS.

under the feudal system, the sachems representing the
petty lords or vassals.

O'bat'in'e'wat, on the Neponset, and the Squaw Sachem, on the Mystic, were the rulers over those whom
the plague had spared in Massachusetts. The Pilgrims
visited the villages of both. All these Indians lived in
great fear of the Tarratines.

When the explorers went back they said that they
wished it had been their lot to have settled at Massachusetts for Plymouth could not be compared with it.

---

[1] MASSACHUSETTS (Indian). The
origin of the name has usually been
referred to the Blue Hills (Roger Williams) as meaning a place of mountains.
It was first given to the country bordering upon Boston Bay only—or between
Nantasket and Port Shirley. Massachusetts Fields was the plain lying on both
sides of the Neponset River.

THE WEYMOUTH COLONY, 1622.

THE influence of the feeble plantation at Plymouth upon emigration was like a little leaven which the woman put into her three pecks of meal.

Thomas Weston, a London merchant, who had been a partner with the Pilgrims, an active, scheming, and

EARLY SETTLEMENTS IN BOSTON BAY.

not over-scrupulous man, thought he saw a better chance for profit in establishing a colony of his own than by continuing to work with his old associates. He therefore separated from them and in 1622 sent about sixty people to begin a settlement in Massachusetts Bay.

In making this selection Weston, no doubt, had in mind the help which the Pilgrims might afford his colonists at need. But the Pilgrims knew from their friends that Weston's men were rude people who had been picked up in the seaports and with whom they would want nothing to do. They however treated the new-comers kindly, giving them food and shelter and medicine for their sick, notwithstanding these bad reports.

Choosing a place which the Indians called Wes´sa´gusset,[1] and the whites later called Weymouth, Weston's men began to build in the midsummer. Though well provided with everything, yet for want of prudent management their provisions began to fail them before harvest time, so that they had to call on their neighbors, the Pilgrims, for help.

Want led to lawlessness. To get food Weston's men would rob the Indians of their corn, which so

GENTLEMAN IN BOOTS.

incensed them that they entered into a league to kill these English.

During the winter many of the settlers died of hunger. Some died while standing on guard. Some sold the clothes off their backs to get food and then went half naked in the bitter winter weather. Some lost all their pride and would fetch wood and water to the Indians, the same as if they had been their servants. At last when they could no longer beg or buy from the Indians, the starving settlers deserted their houses and

scattered themselves in the woods, near the shore, where they could, at least, get clams or groundnuts to eat.

At this time the sachem Aberdecest came with his followers to demand redress for the thefts that had been committed upon his subjects. The whites dared not refuse. So they brought the culprit bound to the sachem to deal with as he saw fit. But Aberdecest spurned the offer. "No," said he indignantly. "Do justice upon him yourselves as Indians do by their bad people." So the man was hanged to appease the wrath of the Indians, and this gave rise to the story that an old and bed-ridden person was hung instead of the real offender.[2]

The Indians now believed the time had come for exterminating all the English. To this end they sent emissaries among their neighbors. They threatened and insulted the starving wretches at Wessagusset whose misery only excited their thirst for revenge.

But in this dark hour the friendship of Massasoit saved them. That king of more than thirty villages fell sick. The Pilgrims sent their friends to minister to his wants. Hearing while on their way to Pokanoket that Massasoit was dead and buried, the Indian guide Hobamok broke out in lamentations. His words were, "My loving sachem! my loving sachem! Many have I known but never any like thee."

When the messengers came into the royal lodge they found the king still alive but sinking fast. With hideous outcries the conjurers were trying to charm the disease away. They told the king that his English friends were come to see him. Massasoit's eyes had grown dim. He feebly asked who had come. They told him it was Winslow. Putting out a thin hand, which Winslow took in his, the dying chieftain said, "Oh Winslow, I shall never see thee again."

But Massasoit did not die. Thanks to Winslow's care he grew better. When he felt his strength returning the king exclaimed, "Now I see the English are my friends and love me; and while I live I will never forget the kindness they have shown me." Then, in gratitude, he told Winslow of the plot hatched by his enemies.

While the Pilgrims were in anxious council over the matter a fugitive was seen coming into the settlement. He had secretly fled from Wessagusset and this was the story he told:

His comrades had learned that the Indians meant to massacre them as well as the English at Plymouth. To warn their neighbors was a duty. All were so far agreed, but no one could be found willing to undertake the perilous journey. Indeed, the Indians watched every movement so closely that to leave the plantation without their

A GROAT.

knowledge seemed impossible. To all intents the settlers were prisoners. Phinehas Pratt however said he would go.

Early the next morning the crafty Peck'su'ot came to the one who had said he would go, and spoke to him thus: "Me hear you go to Patuxet. You will lose yourself. The bears and wolves will eat you. But because I love you I will send my boy Na'ha'mit with you and I will give you victuals to eat by the way and be merry with your friends when you come there."

The messenger saw that he had been betrayed. Putting a bold face upon the matter he said to Pecksuot, "Who told you so great a lie? tell me that I may kill him."

Then Pecksuot sternly answered, "It is no lie. You shall not know." He then drew his blanket round him and stalked away, but immediately after him came five other Indians, who when asked why they came there armed made reply, "We are friends. You carry guns where we dwell, we bring bow and arrows where you dwell."

These savages watched the messenger day and night for seven days. On the eighth he managed to slip away from them into the woods. Knowing that he would be pursued he ran on until his strength gave out, for life and death were in his speed. He had no compass, nor did he know a foot of the way. After wandering in the woods two days and nights he at last reached Plymouth more dead than alive.

CROCK.

The fugitive further said that his comrades were so helpless as to be wholly at the mercy of the savages whenever they should begin the work of slaughter. And he also affirmed that for fear of the savages finding it out when one of them died he was buried in the night by stealth.

The Pilgrims were men of action and this story showed them there was not a moment to lose. They resolved to strike boldly. So they promptly sent Standish to Wessagusset with orders to take summary vengeance, especially upon the cruel Wit´u´wam´at, whose head Standish was charged to bring back to Plymouth.

When Standish came to Wessagusset he found no one

at the settlement, all the men being dispersed abroad, as was said. So Standish announced his arrival with a musket-shot.

Presently an Indian came to spy out Standish's errand. He went back and told his people the English were angry. Then Pecksuot sent word to Standish that he knew the English had come to kill him and his people, "but" said the haughty savage to his messenger, "tell him we fear him not, neither will we shun him. Let him begin when he dare; he will not take us unawares." Others came and would whet their knives and make use of insolent gestures and speeches to Standish's face. Among the rest Wituwamat bragged of the excellence of his knife. He unsheathed it and showed Standish a woman's face carved on the haft. Said he,

"I have another at home with a man's face that hath killed both French and English. By and by this one shall see and by and by it shall eat but not speak. Then they two shall marry."

Then Pecksuot stood forth. Pecksuot was a warrior of huge frame, noted for his great bodily strength. He too had a knife hung round his neck like the others. Addressing Standish he exclaimed with disdain,

"This is the mighty captain the white men have sent to destroy us! He is a little man, let him go and work with the women!"

Standish had only eight men, of whom Hobamok was one. He bore with these taunts until such a time as he could contrive to get Wituwamat and Pecksuot where they could not escape, for with all their boasting they were too cunning to put themselves in the wrathful Captain's power.

One day they boldly came into the house where the Captain was. At a signal from him one of his men fastened the door. Standish then snatched Pecksuot's knife from its sheath and stabbed him to death with it. Wituwamat and another were killed on the spot after a fierce struggle.

When these redoubtable warriors lay dead Hobamok spoke up. "Yonder," said he, "is Pecksuot. Yesterday Pecksuot bragged of his great strength. He said though you were a great captain you were but a little man. To-day I see you are big enough to lay him on the ground."

Several more were shot and one was hanged by Standish's band whom Weston's men had now taken courage and joined. They then went in pursuit of other enemies, but the savages were so thoroughly terrified that they would fly into the swamps whenever they saw Standish coming.

Weston's men now thought only of leaving the settlement. They had a little vessel in the harbor which was used for fishing. In this, most of them embarked for Monhegan where they expected to get passage for home. A few decided to go back with the Plymouth men. Standish saw the departing settlers sail away out of the bay, after which he and his companions returned to Plymouth bringing with them the grisly head of Wituwamat which was stuck on the battlements of their fortress. And thus ended the first settlement in Bostan Bay.[3]

---

[1] Wessagusset (Indian). The site of the settlement is not ascertained. It is supposed to have been on Phillips' Creek, a short distance above Quincy Point Bridge. Robert Gorges, son of Sir Ferdinando, with colonists reoccupied the deserted settlement in the autumn of 1623. He held a commission and assumed authority as governor of New England. They remained through the winter only, some going to Virginia, some back to England.

[2] Consult "New England Legends," p. 365.

[3] Read with this chapter Longfellow's March of Myles Standish.

A LEGEND OF PEDDOCK'S ISLAND.

PEDDOCK'S ISLAND, the one lying out before Nantasket, has a legend, going back of any settlement, which Pecksuot related to the English as follows:

There was a ship broken by a storm. They saved most of their goods and hid them in the ground. We made them tell us where it was. Then we made them our servants. They wept much. When we parted them we gave them such meat as our dogs did eat. One of them had a book he would often read in. We asked him what his book said. He answered, "It saith there will a people come into this country and drive you all away." We took away their clothes. They lived but a little while. One of them lived longer than the rest, for he had a good master who gave him a wife. He is now dead, but hath a son alive.

Another ship came into the bay with much goods to truck. Then I said to the sachem I will tell you how you shall have all for nothing. Bring all our canoes, and all our beaver, and a great many men, but neither bows nor arrows, clubs or hatchets; only knives under the skins about your loins. Throw up much beaver upon their deck. Sell it very cheap and when I give the word thrust your knives in the Frenchmen's bellies. Thus we killed them all. But Monsieur Finch, master of their ship, being wounded, jumped into the hold. We bid him come up, but he would not. Then we cut their cable and the ship went ashore, and lay upon her side, and slept there. Finch came up and we killed him. Then our sachem divided their goods and fired their ship, and it made a very great fire.

NAN'TAS'KET, 1622. Some time in the same year that the plantation was begun at Weymouth a few adventurous Englishmen made themselves a home at the extreme end of the long, hill-crowned peninsula that forms the southernmost headland of Boston Bay. On this miniature Cape Cod they built their lonely cabins. It is still known by its Indian name of Nantasket.

These people were joined (1624–1625) by others whom the Pilgrims had banished from Plymouth for having sown dissensions among them Two of these

A BEGINNING.

refugees, Roger Conant and Rev. John Lyford, very soon went to live at Cape Ann. A third, John Oldham, was the one whose ingenious punishment has been related.

AT WIN'NI'SIM'MET Samuel Maverick built a strongly fortified house in 1625, in which he carried on a trade with the Indians who once assaulted it, but on being repulsed never repeated the attempt. But they repented of their want of courage when they saw so many English come afterward.

AT MISH'A'WUM, a few miles south of where Maverick dwelt, another solitary settler had built himself a rude cabin, thatched and palisaded. His name was Thomas Walford, and he was a smith by trade.

AT SHAW'MUT Rev. William Blackstone lived alone on the heights that rose between the Charles and the next arm of the bay.

AT THOMPSON'S ISLAND, opposite the headland of

Squantum, David Thompson had mad himself a home, probably in 1626. He had been the first settler of New Hampshire, but had removed to Boston Bay out of dislike for his first choice. It is not certainly known in what year Blackstone or Walford settled here, but they are supposed to have belonged to Gorges' company, at Weymouth.

SHAWMUT.

Thus all around Boston, Bay from Winnisimmet on the north, to Nantasket on the south, the smoke of these settlers' cabins rose in sight of each other in the year 1626. And they had picked out the very best points for settlement.

But to complete the chain of settlements in Boston Bay we must now speak of an erratic individual whose career makes the most singular chapter of all.

MORTON OF MERRY-MOUNT, 1625.

CAPTAIN WOLLASTON, of whom very little is known, came in the summer of 1625, with many servants,[1] to start a trading plantation in Massachusetts Bay.

Wollaston did not go to Weston's deserted settlement, though the buildings had been left standing there. One credulous writer says it was because Wollaston believed that the Indian powwows had cast a spell over the place, which rendered it fatal to Englishmen.

In Wollaston's company there was an adventurer by the name of Thomas Morton[2] whose career in New England was a most romantic one. This Thomas Morton was a man of ability and education but he did not bear a good name nor can he with justice be called any

MOUNT WOLLASTON.

thing else than an adventurer of a type common to all new countries.

A little north of Wessagusset was a place which the Indians called Pas'son'a'ges'sit. It is now within the limits of Quincy. The site chosen by Wollaston was a spacious upland rising gently from the beach to the brow of a low hill which still bears its original name of Mount Wollaston. And here the settlers decided to build.

Everything promised well for the undertaking. The Indians had been so thoroughly cowed by Standish that these colonists could have little cause for fear on their account. They built their storehouse on the summit of the hill with the sunny bay and its green islands stretched far out before them, while behind them rose the dark-wooded summits of the Blue Hills.

A single winter's experience seems to have discouraged Captain Wollaston quite in the same way that Weston's and Gorges' men had been before him, for as soon as the spring came he too sailed away for Virginia, taking most of the colonists with him. Over those who were left behind Morton assumed control and he signalized the change of masters by rechristening the place Merry-Mount.

Morton's wild followers resolved to hold high revel in honor of the name. They cut down a tall pine, eighty feet high, for a May-pole, which was brought into the settlement with blowing of horns, beating of drums and firing of guns and pistols, after the old English manner of bringing home the May-pole. A pair of buck's horns were nailed to the top of the pole which was then raised with the help of the savages whom curiosity had brought to the spot. After this a poem composed for the occasion was affixed to the May-pole

> "With proclamation that the First of May
> At Ma-re Mount shall be kept holly day."

Then began a genuine old-fashioned carousal. All comers were invited to help themselves to the ale, strong liquors and other good cheer provided for them and the day ended in the true spirit of bacchanalian revelry, with singing roistering drinking-songs, and dancing round the May-pole,[3] the revellers taking Indian girls for their partners.

When the Pilgrims heard of all this they were greatly scandalized, for they looked upon dancing round a May-

pole as an idolatrous act. Already the evil tendency
of the place as the resort of the idle, profligate and lawless had given them much uneasiness. Then the near-
ness of such neighbors, whose example must in no long
time corrupt the simple natives, give them no pleasant
reflections. But they were in positive terror when they
found that Morton was selling guns to the Indians,—
that he was putting these formidable weapons into the
hands of men who might become enemies any day, the
rather because with guns they would believe themselves
a match for the white men. To make Morton's offence
worse there was a royal proclamation against the sale
of firearms to the Indians which he had broken.

Morton had done this merely to outbid his rivals, in
the trade for beaver-skins. He knew that an Indian
would give any thing he possessed for a gun and he took
advantage of this eager desire. Moreover, he taught
the Indians how to use firearms and then employed
them to hunt for him.

When the Plymouth men saw these hunters ranging
the woods, armed like themselves, they resolved to put
a stop to it at any cost.

They first tried a remonstrance. To this Morton
returned a scornful answer, for he did not love the
"brethren" as he called them any more than they loved
him. Then the people of the half-dozen weak and
scattered plantations that we have named took counsel
of each other how to deal with this evil. The end of it
was a resolution to break up Morton's haunt of free
companions without delay.

This was presently done by Standish who seized
Morton and brought him a prisoner to Plymouth.[4]
Morton stormed and threatened but finding his captors

unmoved he soon grew humble enough. He was shipped off to England to answer the charges against him, but to the dismay of the Pilgrims he was back again in a year to give them still further trouble.

¹ SERVANTS, meaning here persons who sold their time for their outfit, passage, and support.

² THOMAS MORTON was a lawyer. In 1629 he was again banished, his house burned and his May-pole cut down. During his stay in England he printed a book about New England on account of which he was imprisoned when he returned to this country again. Soon after his release he died at Agamenticus (York, Me.).

³ DANCING ROUND A MAY-POLE was held to be a relic of the old Roman festival to the goddess Flora. The custom of going into the woods for flowers is also very ancient.

⁴ MORTON'S ARREST was the occasion of the first combination of the planters of New England.

PIONEERS OF MAINE, 1623–1630.

THE islands about the New England coast were the first known and earliest occupied. Very few had inhabitants: all were natural fortresses that could be assailed only by water and therefore were easily defended.

CRYSTAL HILLS, FROM CAPE ELIZABETH.

Monhegan is foremost of all those islands. Monhegan became to the New England coast what the Azores had been to the mid-Atlantic, not only a place of rendezvous or refreshment, but the one known landmark for which navigators steered.

It is true that New England's greatest landmark was the Crystal Hills, or Twinkling Mountains of Casco, which rose on the edge of the sea before any other land showed itself. An early explorer says of them, "There is no ship arrives in New England, either to the west as far as Cape Cod, or to the east as far as Monhegan, but they see this mountain the first land if the weather be clear."

MONHEGAN ISLAND.

But Monhegan was a familiar word in the mouths of those who sailed the great ocean. Ever since Weymouth's voyage it had been the resort of fishing ships. Ships going to Virginia called there for wood and water. Ships homeward bound stopped there to get cargoes of fish. By and by the people of the scattered plantations resorted to it to buy and sell, to get the news, or receive their letters or take passage for England. So, although without any regular settlement upon it, Monhegan was for years a depot for supplies and resort for intelligence to seafaring men and colonists alike. But fishermen and casual traders are never in the proper sense colonists.

During one severe winter (1619) Monhegan had been the miserable refuge for a band of English mutineers[1] whom their captain had put on shore to shift for themselves. We meet with no other inhabitants except in the fishing seasons until 1623.

The New England coast fishery of those days was carried on mostly by merchants resident in west of England and Channel ports. It had grown to be a great business. Ships left England early in the winter so as to be on our coast by Christmas, if possible, because the winter fishing for cod was by far the best. Therefore there was much rivalry among the masters to be first

A FISHING-SHIP.

at the fishing-grounds, as late comers would find the best places already taken up.

Now if we think of from twenty to thirty or more ships spreading themselves out every year along our Northern New England coast, with their boats at sea and their shoremen busily at work drying the catch on the islands, we shall not only see what life on the coast was like, at that time, but how every creek and harbor of the main must have become well known to these hardy toilers of the sea.

The first thing a fishing-crew had to do was to build a rough platform called a stage, or fishing-room, on which all the work of curing was done. The stage had to be convenient to a landing-place. A frame of stout poles, covered with brushwood, made the stages. At the end of the season they were left standing, as custom gave the earliest comer his choice of stages.

Each ship brought a double crew of men and boys who were divided into fishermen and shoremen. The

LANDING-STAGE.

fishermen went off in the shallops to the fishing-grounds, while the shoremen split, washed, salted, dried and packed the fish ready for shipment.

Of course the shoremen staid mostly on land while making ready the cargo. No long time was needed in which to put up rude shanties, booths or wigwams to shelter themselves in. And these humble dwellings not unfrequently became the kernels of later settlements.

The increasing number of ships frequenting Monhegan led to its purchase (1622) and soon after to the settlement of one or more families upon it. From that time it has a nearly unbroken history.

PEMAQUID POINT[2] was permanently settled as early as 1625.

DAMARISCOVE ISLAND, at the mouth of the Kennebec, was also used as a fishing-station nearly as early as Monhegan was. So were some of the islands in Casco Bay.[3]

All these islands were busy places in summer, for besides landsmen and sailors throngs of

DRYING-FLAKE.

Indians came to barter their beaver-skins for English cloth, blankets, knives or trinkets, or for English guns and rum. But these last could only be obtained of unprincipled traders like Morton. We have seen that Samoset, who was a sachem of Pemaquid, had learned to speak English by holding this sort of intercourse with the sailors.

CARRYING FISH.

We now come to a peculiar feature of Indian life. In the summer season the interior tribes always came in a body to the seashore where they could live easily and sumptuously on fish. Each tribe descended its own river in canoes until they came to the camping-spot which they and their fathers had perhaps frequented for generations. In an hour the squaws would build wigwams enough

to shelter the band. These places of resort are known to-
day by the shell-mounds made by successive generations
of Indians during their annual excursions. Some are

WASHING FISH.

very extensive.
The greatest in
New England
are those situat-
ed on the Dam-
ariscotta River.
Yet, notwith-
standing their
wandering habits, no people have ever had greater love
for their native land than the American Indians.

[1] MUTINEERS put ashore at Saco by
Captain Rocroft.
[2] PEMAQUID POINT; by John Brown.

[3] CHRISTOPHER LEVETT built on an
island in Portland harbor in 1623, but
abandoned it the same year.

PIONEERS OF MAINE—*Continued.*

ALTHOUGH Sir Ferdinando Gorges had hired Richard
Vines with a few men to stay at Saco during the winter
of the plague and Vines had since carried on some
trade with the Indians there, no actual permanent settlement was effected between the Kennebec and Piscataqua before 1630. It was then begun at nearly the same
time by Vines and others at Saco[1] and by Edward Godfrey[2] and others—all under Gorges' authority—at
Agamenticus, now York.

Meanwhile the Pilgrims had quietly pushed on their
plans for controlling the Indian trade in several direc-
tions. In 1628 they established a trading-post on the
Kennebec, where, indeed, they had been trading with

the Indians for several years. Two years later, they had started another house on the Penobscot.[3]

From 1623 to 1630 is a period of almost inaction so far as colonization is concerned. In order to know why such men as Gorges and Mason made no greater efforts in this direction we must look to England.

An angry warfare was going on there between king and Parliament over the kingly prerogative. James had publicly declared that he would govern for the good of the common weal and not according to the common will. Granting royal charters to favorites was one of the abuses of power at which the people grumbled the most. Consequently Parliament, as the voice of the people, had declared against all the great monopolies that the king had created. Gorges was then fighting

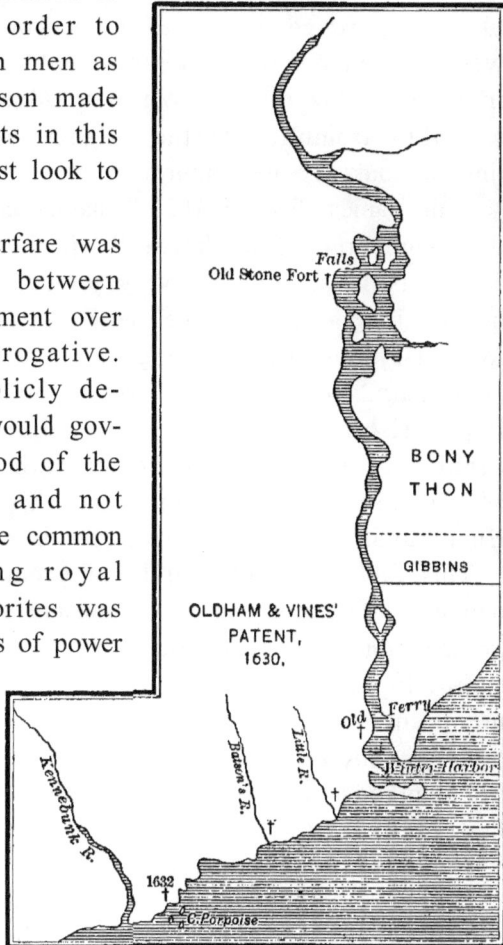

SACO AND CAPE PORPOISE SETTLEMENTS.

hand to hand with Parliament for the life of the New England Charter which, before all the rest, had been adjudged a public grievance. James, it is true, stood by Gorges, as he was bound to do, but inasmuch as the real blow was aimed at the arbitrary king, so Parliament went on and recorded its judgement against the charter in spite of his threats. While the fate of the charter was thus trembling in the balance, it surely was no time to make greater outlays or plan new schemes.

King James died in 1625. Charles became king, with the plague raging so dreadfully in London that it was said a bell was tolling every minute. Charles had inherited his father's quarrel with Parliament and added to it. He soon involved England in a war with France and Spain. To carry on these unpopular wars he was impoverishing the people with oppressive exactions. Finally in the town of Portsmouth, where Captain Mason commanded for the king, his odious favorite Buckingham [4] had been assassinated.

This fatality closed a train of events which had left neither Gorges nor Mason the leisure to attend to their private concerns beyond the seas.

But in 1629 Charles abruptly dissolved the Parliament and this time it did not reassemble, it being mostly composed of Puritans who would not yield to his demands and for whom he had a strong dislike. Out of this troubled state of things came the great Puritan emigration to New England.

With the king as their champion and Parliament silenced Gorges and Mason were now free to pursue their plans, which they immediately began doing with vigor, but they meant to build up only such communities as would be loyal to the king and to the Established

Church of England, for to both the Puritans were hostile.

So now Gorges began his settlements at Saco and Agamenticus, while Mason began his on the Pis'cat'a'-qua, of which we shall speak presently.

The settlement at Agamenticus was so situated as to lend a hand to, or receive help from, its neighbors on the Piscataqua, but had no such natural resources at its command. It took its name from the solitary mountain that is the conspicuous landmark far and near. Subsequently it was called Gorgeana in honor of Gorges, but it never grew to be the great or populous city its founders had desired it should, because its natural position was inferior both as a port and as an outlet for the interior country. Yet it must be borne in mind that Saco, Agamenticus and Piscataqua were chosen centres for colonization after more than twenty years' exploration and experience.

To the region embraced within his grant Gorges gave the name of Maine[5] and he is rightly called its founder.

[1] SACO was the first seat of government, it being the most important, as well as the oldest, settlement within the Gorges patent. Vines first acted as governor over the scattered plantations between the Piscataqua and Kennebec. Six years later, Gorges sent his nephew William Gorges to establish *de facto* government in his province, which was formally done by convening the principal inhabitants in a court held at Saco in March 1636. It was a proprietary government giving Gorges all powers except those touching the fealty of the subject, and under it the Church of England was made the legal form of worship. All officers, civil or military, were either appointed by the proprietor or confirmed by him. The local governor was his agent. The system was the opposite of that established in Massachusetts and in no sense was it a popular form. Gorges himself admitted his failure to people his province with actual settlers.

[2] EDWARD GODFREY was for many years an active promoter of settlement in new England. He built the first house at Agamenticus, or York.

[3] PENOBSCOT. *See* chart, p.102.

[4] BUCKINGHAM. Look this incident up in your English history. It is historically important.

[5] MAINE, supposed to be so named from a department of France, though why it should be is not clear. Some have supposed it derived from the word "main" or main land. But this is hardly probable, not only because it would lack meaning but was at variance with the custom of the time.

THE ISLES OF SHOALS.[1]

SEVEN bald crags rise out of the sea on the New Hampshire coast like the tips of sunken mountains, but lately submerged. These isles are broken into great jagged cliffs against which the sea roars and breaks in clouds of spray and foam. On some a little grass grows among the rocks and more sheltered hollows, but all are so bleak and desolate, so swept by the wild wind and waves, that no one would think of them as a place of abode. Still, they have been long occupied and by quite a numerous population and are now a favorite summer resort.

ISLES OF SHOALS.

> "A heap of bare and splintery crags
>   Tumbled about by lightning and frost,
> With rifts and chasms and storm-bleached jags
>   That wait and growl for a ship to be lost."[2]

These almost naked rocks are the Isles of Shoals. They are the natural seamark for the entrance to the Piscataqua, yet lie so low in the water as to have been rocks of danger to early navigators. So that tales of shipwreck are not wanting to invest the islands with a kind of romantic interest.

They were seen by Champlain and probably by Gosnold and Pring[3] before him, for in clear weather no ship can come near this coast without sighting them.

After these navigators came Captain Smith who named the group Smith's Isles,[4] for himself, but the present name very soon took the place of his, though it is not certain how it originated.

These islet-peaks emerge from the sea in the form of a crater into which the sea has poured, making a little harbor it the midst of it. To this one little haven they owe all their importance in history.

For like Monhegan the Isles of Shoales became the resort of fishing-ships early in the seven-

STONE CHURCH, STAR ISLAND.

teenth century. We do not hear however of their being made use of until settlement began on the Piscataqua, when six ships fished there the same year. But so inhospitable did the islands appear that for a long time no one seems to have thought of settling upon them. And even the time when they were settled is in doubt.[5] Fishermen first inhabited them—rough fellows owning to so little law or morals, except their own rude code, that women were forbidden to go upon the islands. When a minister went among them he went as a missionary goes to the heathen of other lands, for living as they did, apart from their fellow-men, the islanders seemed almost to have forgotten the habits of civilization.

In time this condition of things mended, but the islanders always seemed to partake somewhat of the wildness of their island home.

[1] ISLES OF SHOALS, viz. Appledore, Star, Smutty-Nose, Cedar, White, Londoner's and Duck. They were granted to Gorges and Mason, therefore now partly in Maine and partly in New Hampshire.
[2] LOWELL'S "Pictures from Appledore."

[3] MARTIN PRING made a voyage of discovery to this coast, 1603.
[4] SMITH'S ISLES. A monument on Star Island commemorates his name.
[5] NO TRACE is found of a settlement until after 1630.

PIONEERS OF NEW HAMPSHIRE, 1623–1629.

"God save Englonde and the Towne of Rye."—Old Customal.

WHAT is now New Hampshire received its first colonists in the spring of 1623 when David Thompson[1] with a small company began at Odiorne's Point, in what is now Rye, a settlement which he designed for a fishing and trading post. It took the name of Piscataqua[2] from the river on which it was located.

Here Thompson built a large and strong house which he surrounded with a high palisade, for there was no other white man nearer than fifty miles by land or water. But with stout hearts and plenty of ammunition the New England pioneer felt as secure in his wooden castle as any baron of old did in his mountain fortress.

He showed much judgment in choosing as he did. The river on which he had planted himself was supposed to run a long way through the wilderness country. Of course this meant a natural highway for the Indians to bring beaver to him. The best of harbors was near, the sea lay at his doors and the Isles of Shoals were in full view from his windows.

The site too was admirably chosen. It is a little rising ground near the Odiorne homestead of to-day. Part of the walls, with the great chimney-stack rising out of the ruins, stood for many years, but now not one stone remains upon another to show where the first house in New Hampshire was built.

But quite near the homestead are a few sunken, un-lettered headstones which are supposed to mark the graves of some of the early settlers. They have outlasted every vestige of wall or palisade.

We think of Thompson as being a hermit in his loneliness and seclusion. But he had scarcely reared his abode before

THE PISCATAQUA SETTLEMENTS.

his neighbors began to pay him friendly visits.

One of the first to seek his hospitality was the once prosperous patron of the Pilgrims, Mr. Weston, who now came a miserable fugitive in rags. Quitting England in disguise, to avoid arrest, he heard at Monhegan of the ruin that had befallen his colony. With two men he at once set sail in a shallop for Wessagusset and it was while trying to get there that a storm had driven his boat on shore. Narrowly escaping death from the waves Weston fell into the hands of the Indians who stripped him and then let him go. In this plight he made his way to Thompson's house and shortly after to Plymouth, a beggar among those whom he had once scornfully told that "they were now quit of him and he of them."

Next came Robert Gorges who had come to New England with so much authority and so little experience, to found a capital city.

GRAVES OF THE SETTLERS.

Myles Standish was another visitor. He had come seeking help for a long continued drought was threatening the Pilgrims with famine. Thompson generously gave the Plymouth captain what he could spare and then went back with him to Plymouth.

So we see friendly intercourse springing up between these isolated settlements as common interest dictated.

Besides Thompson's, another party had gone higher up the stream to a place where the river divides, enclosing a beautiful peninsula. They made a settlement here, which is generally believed to be nearly, if not quite, as early as Thompson's, and was called Hilton's Point[3] from the name of one of its founders. These were also fishermen and traders Possibly they meant to intercept the Indians who should come down the river to trade with Thompson.

For the next few years scarcely any thing is heard of these two little plantations. We know that Thompson's did not flourish because he removed to Boston Bay in 1626. Of the Hiltons we know even less. But though feeble, we think both settlements were permanent.

Six years after Thompson built his house, Captain John Mason [4] took a patent in his own name for all the country lying between the Merrimack and Piscataqua as far back as sixty miles from the coast. To this tract the name of New Hampshire [5] was given.

---

[1] DAVID THOMPSON was a Scottish gentleman who was associated with certain Plymouth (Eng.) merchants.

[2] PISCATAQUA (Indian) means a branching of the river.

[3] HILTON's POINT is now in Dover, N.H.

[4] CAPTAIN JOHN MASON founder of New Hampshire had been governor of Newfoundland where he became well acquainted with the needs of new colonies and with maritime affairs generally. Died 1635, after incurriug heavy losses in his colonial schemes.

[5] NEW HAMPSHIRE named for Hampshire, a shire of England.

PIONEERS OF NEW HAMPSHIRE—*Continued.*

THE next year (1630) Captain Walter Neal[1] was sent over to govern Mason's province, and very soon after other colonists, of whom some were stewards, some artificers, some laborers and some women, went to join him. Arms and artillery, farming and building tools, clothing and stores of all kinds were generously provided; as also were goats, swine and Danish cattle of high breed.

Neal was a soldier of fortune who had lived much in camps. He was charged to find the great lakes of which the Indians told such highly colored stories—how they were beautiful beyond description, teeming with beaver, and swarming with fish and game. Mason supposed that the Piscataqua led directly to this lake region, and that once he had opened the way to it all its wealth would flow into his hands, instead of going to the Dutch at New Amsterdam.

So Neal set about discovering those lakes. They were reckoned at a hundred miles' distance from the seacoast which shows us that Neal probably had taken one great lake for another—Win´ni´pi´se´o´gee[2] for Champlain. Mason had heard of Champlain's great lake of the Iroquois. Neal heard the Indians who came down the Piscataqua continually talking about their great lake, lying at so many days' journey into their country.

For want of provisions to go on, Neal's party had to turn back when they supposed themselves to be within a day's march of the lakes. So Mason's prime object was frustrated.

Within a year the two original settlements had increased to four.

About three miles distant from the mouth of the river the west shore rises into a low promontory which the settlers called Strawberry Bank on account of the profusion of strawberries growing wild upon it.[3]

At this point the stream suddenly broadens into a spacious basin, with deep and rapid tide, yet securely landlocked by islands. No better harborage could be found. Here, at this place, in 1631, Humphrey Chadbourne built for the proprietors what presently took the name of the Great House,[4] from which the city of Portsmouth has sprung.

The fourth settlement was begun at the same time by Ambrose Gibbins, another of the company's agents, who built a trading-house some miles higher up the river than Hilton's Point, at a place which the Indians called Ne'wich'wan'nock. [5] It had been chosen on account of the falls there which not only made it convenient for intercepting the Indians and for erecting saw-mills which Mason meant to do by and by, but because it was the head of tide navigation.

Ambrose Gibbins' palisaded house was for several years the solitary outpost of all this region. A little way above him were the Salmon Falls where many generations of Indians had speared the salmon. With his family and a few hired men to help him Gibbins bravely held this little spot of wilderness ground until other settlers came to his aid. What such a life as his was is best told in his own words:

"For myself my wife and child and four men we have but half a barrel of corn. Beefe and porke I have not had but one peese this three months, nor bear this four months; for I have for two and twenty months had but two barrels of beare and two barrels and four booshel of malt. Our number commonly hath been ten. I nor the servants have neither money nor clothes. . . . You may perhaps think that fewer men would serve me but I have sometimes one hundred or more Indians and far from neybors."

We thus see how natural it is for settlements to follow up the course of rivers and that rivers are to a country what charts of genealogy are to a family. This Piscataqua River had its highest sources in the hunting-grounds of the Ossipee tribes who for an unknown time had followed it in making their annual excursions to the sea.

Meanwhile the settlement at Little Harbor, or Odiorne's Point, had extended itself to Great Island, as Newcastle was first called. At the southeast corner of this island, on the present site of Fort Constitution, a fort was built and armed. It is also thought that a few straggling settlers had built their cabins along the northern shore of the river, at Kittery Point, Spruce Creek and in Eliot.

The colony remained three years under Neal's care. In that time four townships were laid out which were named by Mason's order Portsmouth, Northam, Hampton, and Exeter, the two last not yet being settled. While doing this, Great and Little Boar's Head were named by Neal.

OLD FORT, NEWCASTLE.

At the end of these three years Neal went back to England in order to give an account of his stewardship to the company of proprietors of whom Mason was the head. He did not again return to New England where, as plain-speaking Ambrose Gibbins told his employers, "the great looks of men and many words" would not suffice to build up a plantation.

For ten years after their beginning all these Piscataqua plantations depended on England and Virginia for the bread they ate. Little attention was paid to raising crops although the settlers wrote home that the soil was well-adapted to agriculture. Yet notwithstanding these reports the energies of the proprietors were wholly given to getting beaver, fish and lumber—in other words to stripping the country of its natural products rather than to rendering their plantations self-sustaining. It was a most unwise policy for the good of the country, but these proprietors looked more to enriching themselves than to making homes for those who should come after them. Give us what we can turn into money and we will send you supplies was their standing order. The result was that their people often stood on the verge of starvation, like Ambrose Gibbins, and that instead of being able to take care of themselves at the end of six years, and have corn to sell, like the Pilgrims, at the end of ten these planters were still being fed from home at great cost and trouble. They had cattle and goats and swine which helped them to subsist in a measure, but with the head in England the body could not and did not thrive three thousand miles away.

So while the Pilgrims were working like beavers for themselves, Mason's men were simply working for their masters in England. And again, while the Pilgrims were making a living on much poorer soil, the New Hampshire settlers were getting grain from Virginia, and then sending it a hundred miles to Boston to be ground.

[1] CAPTAIN NEAL spent most of his time in exploring and surveying. After his recall the proprietors did not again employ him.

[2] WINNIPISEOGEE, now pronounced as if spelt Winnepesawkee. Noted fishing, trapping and hunting place.

[3] STRAWBERRY BANK extended from the South Mill-Pond to the river, taking in what is now Church Hill.

[4] THE GREAT HOUSE etood near the corner of Court and Water streets.

[5] NEWICHWANNOCK (Indian). Now South Berwick, Me. Indian name of falls was Quampeagan, said to mean "fishing-place weir."

CAPE ANN, 1624.

THE Pilgrims being in a sense a trading company, bound by articles of association to their English partners, they much desired to profit by the coast fisheries which were making so many others rich while they continued poor with the fishing-grounds at their very doors. Their partners strongly urged them to do this, and promised to furnish ships for the purpose.

So thinking that to be a good place, they hit upon Cape Ann for a fishing and trading station. Plymouth was too far from the fishing-grounds and its harbor none of the best.

Cape Ann is a long granite ledge, or series of ledges,

CAPE ANN.

thrust out from the mainland and dividing the ocean into two considerable basins. Enclosed in its outermost headland is a good harbor, with bold shores into which the sea has worn many little coves, that form natural landing places. As we have already learned Prince Charles named this promontory Cape Ann.

The first fishing-ship which came to Plymouth was sent to Cape Ann in the spring of 1624, to begin fishing

there. Some of the Pilgrims went in her to help build
a house and stages. They chose the high bluff in
Gloucester harbor, which has ever since borne the name
of Stage Head.[1]

Though much was expected from the venture very
little came from it. The ship came late, her master
proved incompetent, and her crew were ungovernable.
Still, what was then done at Cape Ann laid the foundation for its future prosperity.

The next season, the Pilgrims sent their salt-maker,
with others, to begin the manufacture of salt at Cape
Ann, but through his carelessness the house that had
been built there the year before took fire and was burnt
to the ground, and so that enterprise fell through.

By this time, owing to continual failures, the English
partners[2] had become dissatisfied with the whole business, and withdrew their support from the Pilgrims.
There were factions in the company at home and factions among the colonists themselves. Some of the merchants then sent out a ship of their own to fish at Cape
Ann. When it arrived there the crew took possession
of the stage belonging to the Pilgrims. Hearing of this
the Pilgrims sent Standish to demand it of them, which
he did on the spot. The intruders made a barricade of
hogsheads, posted themselves behind it with arms, and
defied Standish to come and take it from them. High
words passed. From words they would no doubt have
come to blows, for Standish's hot blood was now up, if,
fortunately, Conant had not been there to act as mediator in the dispute. The trouble ended with the Pilgrims giving up fishing at Cape Ann altogether, which
they were the more willing to do because the business
had been a losing one for them from the beginning.

Meanwhile, the failure of the fishing enterprise had led the Rev. John White[3] and some other persons of ability and foresight to conclude that the only way to succeed was by planting a permanent colony. With some one on the spot to govern it, and with a missionary to aid in the work, the lawless fishermen might become law-abiding and even devout settlers. It differed from the Pilgrims' plan only in keeping the control in England, while the Pilgrims governed themselves.

These persons, who

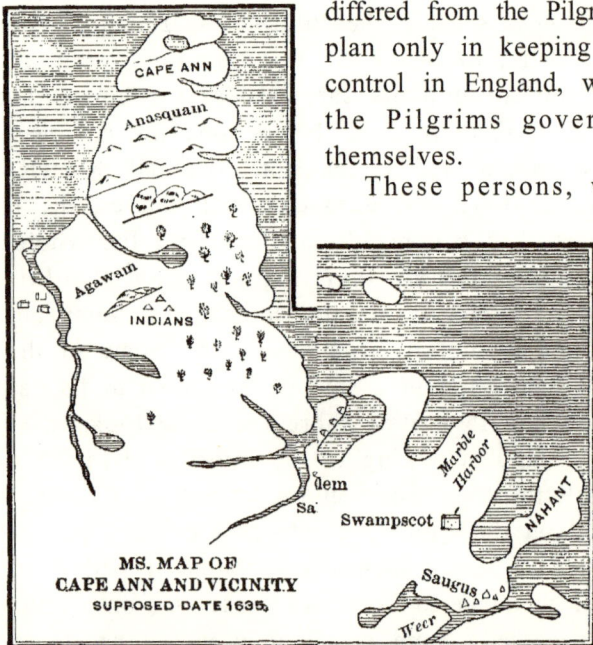

MS. MAP OF
CAPE ANN AND VICINITY
SUPPOSED DATE 1635.

chiefly resided in Dorchester, England, invited Roger Conant [4] to come and manage their affairs for them at Cape Ann. They knew him to be a man of worth who had a knowledge of the country. Conant accepted. They also asked Lyford to settle at Cape Ann as their minister. He too accepted, and both he and Conant removed from Nantasket to enter upon their charge at Cape Ann.

It was the old story over again. Conant found himself powerless to restrain the lawless men that the company had sent out: while the company upon finding the project was a losing one gave it up in discouragement after only a year's trial.

Most of the colonists went home in the company's ships, but Conant being a resolute man determined to hold his ground until such time as men and means could be sent to him; for Mr. White had promised that if Conant would stay, this should surely be done. Conant, therefore, led the handful of men who continued faithful, in search of a less unfertile place of residence, and farther back on the mainland, on a peninsula which the Indians called Naumkeag, he found a place more suitable for settlement.

Weary with waiting his men often urged him to go with them to Virginia; but Conant told them that even if they should all forsake him he would stay there alone.

This was how Roger Conant came to build the first house (1626) in what is now the city of Salem of which he must be considered the founder.

---

[1] STAGE HEAD is the traditional location.

[2] ENGLISH PARTNERS. Some of them were Churchmen who did not relish the idea of helping to build up a Separatist Church. On this account they prevented the old pastor, Robinson, as well as the rest of the Leyden people, from going over to their friends. They even sent out a minister in their own interest; and in other ways threw obstacles in the way of strengthening the Pilgrim Church. This caused trouble. Moreover their business relations were never harmonious.

[3] REV. JOHN WHITE, a Puritan minister most active in promoting emigration. Author of the "Planter's Plea."

[4] ROGER CONANT, already mentioned as banished from Plymouth. (See Nantasket.) Entire silence is observed by the Pilgrims as to the cause. Bradford does not mention him at all. Hubbard gives him an excellent character. He is supposed to have been a moderate Puritan, but not a Separatist. Governor's Island in Boston harbor was first called Conant's. Conant went from Salem to Beverly and died there in 1679. His son was the first white child born in Salem.

INDIAN TRAITS.

INDIAN SHREWDNESS. As is well known the Indians have been removed farther and farther from their homes to make room for the whites. Once, when an agent of the government was sent to a certain tribe to notify them that they must again remove, a chief asked the agent to sit down on a log. The agent did so. The chief then asked him to move, and very soon to move again, and again, until the agent got to the end of the log. The Indian then said "Move farther."—"I cannot" replied the agent. "Just so it is with us" said the chief. "You have moved us as far as we can go and then ask us to move still farther."

WAMPUM AND ITS MEANING. Among the New England Indians the manufacture and use of wampum, or shell money, seems to have begun with the Narragansetts who sold it to the whites, who again used it the same as money in buying furs of the Eastern Indians, by whom wampum came to be highly prized. In short it represented the wealth of a tribe.

But wampum had for the Indian a higher meaning. Beautifully wrought, the belts, or strings, of shells, stood not only as his highest work of art and workmanship, but were his records, his tokens, or pledges, of friendship, or his credentials to other peoples or tribes.[1]

As we have said in the first chapter the Indians had no written records. Belts of wampum were usually exchanged between tribes to ratify treaties of peace or war or as pledges of the good faith of the parties. Hence they not only bore a character of sacredness, but symbolized the whole history of a war, a great council, or other remarkable event in the history of a tribe. We should now call this object teaching. No two belts were exactly alike. Some are very beautiful indeed and show the Indian's appreciation of art, as the idea of the belt itself does the poetic side of his nature.

At certain seasons the Indians used to meet in order to study the meaning and renew the memories of the wampum belts. Seated in a circle, the belts were passed from hand to hand, while the story of each was being repeated by the old men of the tribe. In this way what each belt stood for was made familiar to old and

KING PHILIP'S WAMPUM BELT.

young. Boys who were the sons of chiefs were admitted to these talks in order that they might get acquainted with the concerns of their tribe at an age when such things impress themselves most. Wampum also was sometimes given in pledge for private friendship. There is no instance of such a promise ever having been broken by an Indian.

Wampum was made from the inner wreath of the cockle or periwinkle, some shells being white and others blue, veined with purple. The white beads were used by the Indians for stanching the flow of blood from a wound. Its commercial value differed as much as gold and silver, being first determined by the quality and next by its workmanship. In trade the strings passed at so much a fathom. Having little gold and silver the whites soon adopted wampum as a medium of trade.

INSCRIPTIONS. So far as known, the New England Indians made but sparing use of hieroglyphics, or symbols, to convey intelligence or embody history. The remarkable bowlder known as Dighton Rock,[2] so long claimed as the work of the Northmen, is the solitary example of this kind. Though its meaning cannot now be deciphered, there is little room for doubt that it was the work of the aborigines.

INDIAN AUTOGRAPH.

Sometimes a hunting or war party, when it became separated, would make rude drawings on the bark of trees in order to inform their friends of their success, or the direction they had taken. Individuals had their own mark, or sign-manual, sometimes of a favorite animal, but oftener derived from prowess in war or the chase, which was affixed to written documents of the white men—such as deeds of land or treaties. But among themselves the Indians never used such things.

WEAPONS AND IMPLEMENTS. These were of stone, rarely of metal, nearly identical with those used by the barbarous peoples of Europe during what is called the Stone Age. England, like America, was civilized by the incoming of strangers.

BURIAL RITES. The New England Indians buried their dead. In other parts of the country they were placed on scaffolds or in trees to protect them from wild beasts, showing the existence of a wholly different train of ideas with respect to the disposal of the body. Again, our Indians always buried in a sitting posture instead of laying the remains in a recumbent position, as was done by some tribes. Putting the dead warrior's arms, trinkets, earthen pots, with a little store of dried maize by his side was a custom common to all, for all believed in a resurrection of the body and a future state in which he would have need of these things. Burial places on a large scale were unfrequent. One such, from which several skeletons have been taken, is found on the western shore of Ossipee Lake, N. H. Princes were sometimes buried in enclosures, made of palisades, but in general no mark of a place of sepulture was left, for though the funeral rite of a warrior was celebrated with much feasting and lamentation there was no after period of mourning, and even to mention a

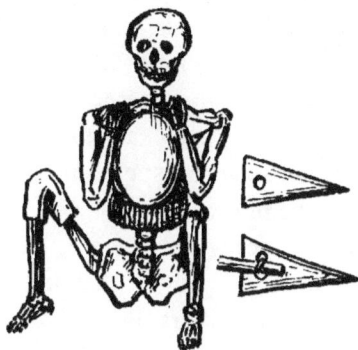

SKELETON AND WEAPONS EXHUMED AT FALL RIVER.

dead person by name was held an offence among them, as tending to weaken the hearts of the living.

COUNCILS. These were always opened by smoking and conducted with the greatest gravity and deliberation. Only chiefs took part in important councils. When one rose to speak he was listened to without interruption. When he sat down a long silence ensued in order that his words might be properly weighed by those present. Great deference was paid to what their old men said. No greater breach of decorum could possibly occur than for a warrior to jump to his feet until his turn came, or interrupt as speaker until he was through. I have known three-quarters of an hour to pass without a word being spoken.

Most Indians are natural orators and the language they sometimes employed to express their thoughts was very striking and appropriate, as will be seen by the following account of the ceremony of burying the hatchet, as the making of peace with their enemies was called by the Indians.

On this occasion one of the chiefs arose and proposed that a large oak which grew near by should be torn up by the roots in order that the hatchet might be buried underneath it, where it might remain forever.

After he had sat down, another, who was greatly revered, rose to speak in his turn. Said he, "Trees may be overthrown by storms, and in course of time will certainly decay. Therefore, that the hatchet may forever be at rest, I advise that it be buried under the high mountain which rears its proud head behind yonder forest."

This proposal greatly pleased the whole assembly till an aged chief, distinguished for his wisdom, rose and gave his opinion in the following remarkable words: "Look upon me! I am but a poor, feeble old man and have not the irresistible power of the Great Spirit to tear up trees by the roots, or overthrow mountains. But if you would forever hide the hatchet from our sight let it be cast into the Great Lake where no man can find it or bring it forth to raise enmity between us and our white brethren."

The Indians always spoke of these assemblies as Council-Fires because it was their custom to light great fires in the council-house when one was being held.

Then the chief who was to speak for his tribe would rise and address the other party in this manner:

"We are come to join two bodies into one."

"We are come to learn wisdom of you brothers." Giving a belt.

"We, by this belt, wipe away the tears of your friends whose relations have been killed; and the paint from your soldiers' faces." Giving another belt.

"We now throw aside the axe, which was put into our hands, by third belt."

After these formalities were over the matter in hand was taken up.

Having no other record of solemn treaties than the help of memory, with the aid given it by certain distinguishing belts, the Indian orator generally took to the council a handful of sticks one of which he would hand to some chief whose duty it then became to remember the particular article of the treaty which was being discussed. As the conference went on the orator gave away his sticks one by one. Much to the astonishment of the whites the Indians were thus able to repeat all that had been said at a previous council.

DECLARATION OF WAR. This was called by the Indians "digging up the hatchet" as to "bury the hatchet" signified ending a war. They always made use of certain solemnities. First there was a great council at which the matter was discussed in all its bearings. Then the conjurers were called upon to foretell the result. When war was decided upon the tribe usually had a great feast, followed by a war-dance, in which every warrior took part. At these dances the warriors would work themselves up to the highest pitch of frenzy. A stout post, called a war-post, was planted in the cen-

tre of the village. Around this the braves who meant
to go to war ranged themselves with their hatchets in
their hands.   They then began to chant their war-songs,
while the boys and squaws beat time on rude drums to
the wild measure of the dance. Each warrior advanced
in turn to the post and struck his hatchet into it as if
he were cleaving the skull of an enemy. He boasted of
his former deeds and of the number of scalps he was
going to take. If one of their own braves had been
killed they believed his spirit would not rest until they
had taken revenge. Their chiefs who wanted war sought
to excite the backward ones by inflammatory appeals.
Said they "The bones of your murdered countrymen
lie uncovered. They cry aloud to us for revenge and
it is our duty to obey them. Their spirits call to us
and we must satisfy them. Let us go in pursuit of the
murderers of our brethren! Do not sit idle! Rise
up and follow the impulse of your valor! Sharpen
your hatchets! Paint your faces so that your enemies
will be afraid to look upon you! Fill your quivers!
Make the woods echo with your voices! Comfort the
spirits of the dead with the blood of your enemies!"

[1] TOKENS. Much the same idea is embodied here as in the use of signets by the ancient Jews, Assyrians and Greeks to accredit a messenger.

[2] DIGHTON ROCK. The claim of pre-Columbian antiquity for this inscription has now been practically abandoned by those most interested in establishing it as the work of their countrymen.

IV.

COMING OF THE PURITANS.

THE COLONY AT SALEM.

STEP by step we have traced the footprints of the pioneers. We have seen the day feebly breaking over the infant settlements. The world had waited long for the dawning, but at last the sun was rising in full splendor above the horizon of New England.

At this time it is thought that in all New England there were about three hundred English settlers.

True to his promise, the Rev. John White had exerted himself to such purpose that he speedily enlisted many knights, gentlemen, and merchants in his humane project. He or they had conceived the idea of making in New Eng-

SALEM AND VICINITY.

149

land a retreat for those persecuted English Puritans who preferred exile to tyranny at home. What the Pilgrims had done could surely be done again.

Of course most of those who promised help were themselves Puritans at heart and so in sympathy with this design. But they had to use great care and tact.

Without delay, these gentlemen sought a grant of the country lying between the Charles and Merrimack rivers, to which, notwithstanding all the failures to set-

OLD HOUSE WITH GABLES, SALEM, MASS.

tle it, they still looked as the choicest part of New England. The Plymouth Company, by its council, readily granted what was asked, and from this time forth the new associates took the name of the Massachusetts Company.

This was in 1628. Within three months the Company had got ready one little ship with about a hundred colonists destined for New England. This little band was going to try the experiment of the Mayflower over again.

The next thing was to choose a leader to govern

these people. The Company looked about them for the most fit man and their choice fell upon Captain John Endicott,[1] who was one of their own members. When asked if he would go out to New England, he said with decision that he would. Having put his affairs in order Endicott took his wife and children on board the Abigail. All being ready she set sail late in June, and early in September (1628) she arrived at Naumkeag.

Endicott found Conant and his trusty companions waiting for him. In the Company's name he took for-

ROGER WILLIAMS' HOUSE, SALEM, MASS.

mal possession of the lands, houses[2] and boats belonging to the old Cape Ann fishing company, and then he and his people earnestly set about preparing homes for themselves before winter should overtake them.

The Indians who dwelt in this neighborhood belonged to the Agawam tribe. Their sagamore's residence was at Ipswich and his name was Masconomo.

From these Indians Conant had received no harm. On the contrary, they often came to him for food, shelter or help when the Tarratines made war upon them, as they usually did in the harvest season; for these Tarratines were fiercer and more warlike than the Agawams and they preferred making spoil of their neighbors to tilling the soil for themselves. When making one of these raids they would steal unperceived along the shores in their canoes to within a short march of the Agawams' village, then landing under cover of the darkness they would hide themselves in the forest until daybreak and then with wild war-whoops would sally forth upon the unsuspecting Agawams and put them to flight.

This shows us why the Indians could never combine together to drive off the English, when they were so few. It was because the Indians were divided by very ancient feuds, which had lasted from generation to generation. But they had never heard the fable of the cony and the hedgehog.[3] So the Agawams gladly gave the English leave to settle upon their lands.

One of the first things that Endicott did was to go across the bay to Merry-Mount and cut down Morton's May-pole. After warning Morton's men to behave themselves better in future Endicott left them to reflect upon what had happened.

We are not informed how Endicott's people passed their first winter but judge it to have been a leaf taken from the Pilgrims' experience. The same fatal sickness, which in every case had proved the colonist's worst enemy, also broke out at Naumkeag. Endicott wrote to Governor Bradford for a physician[4] who was promptly sent and warmly welcomed.

In the early summer (1629) the Company sent over two hundred more colonists who arrived at Naumkeag the last of June. With them came three Puritan min-

isters [5] whom the Company had engaged. They also
sent word to Endicott of his formal election as governor
over the colony and also forwarded to him a copy of
their patent, with its broad seal attached; with direc-
tions to organize his government.

These new-comers found about ten houses already
built, one being "a fair new house for the governor."
They saw cornfields planted, and horses, cattle and
goats quietly grazing in the wild pastures around the
little plantation. They had arrived at a most delightful
season when every thing wore its most attractive aspect,
and were in raptures with all they saw—so much so,
indeed, that some of them imprudently wrote home exaggerated accounts of the country.

These planters now called their settlement Salem [6]
from the Hebrew word meaning "peace." They found
good clay and set up a brick-kiln, for the first bricks
used had been brought over in the ships they came in;
they also began trading, felling timber, surveying lands,
and exploring, like men who expected to make the country their home.

The Company had directed Endicott to take and hold
possession of other places so as to shut out rival claim-
ants. He therefore sent one party to the Charles River,
where we remember that older settlers had already
found a home. When they came to Mishawum, they
found Walford, the smith, dwelling quite contentedly
among the Indians there in a thatched and palisaded
cabin. With the consent of Sagamore John, chief of
that place, Endicott's men began a settlement which
presently (1629) took the name of Charlestown, from
the river Charles that flowed before it.

During this summer Endicott's colony also gathered

their first church. On the appointed day the colonists all came together and with fitting solemnity chose Samuel Skelton their pastor and Francis Higginson their teacher. This was the first completely organized Puritan Church [7] in New England.

Their second winter was one of even greater trial than the first had been. The colonists were again wasted by an infectious disease brought among them by

FIRST MEETING-HOUSE, SALEM, MASS.

persons who had contracted it on shipboard. Eighty died. The rest were mostly weak and sick, with destitution staring them in the face. So that in the following summer the colony offered a sad, dispiriting sight to its new-come friends.

But Endicott was a man of Roman stamp and a worthy successor to sturdy Roger Conant. Moreover he knew that great preparations were on foot to sustain him and his colony.

¹ JOHN ENDICOTT was a man of iron will and great individuality. Naturally a leader and a Puritan of the sternest type he is found not only always on the aggressive side, but in the forefront of every movement signalling the somewhat arbitrary policy of the Puritan Fathers toward religious opponents. Though holding such extreme views Endicott was often put by the people in the highest office within their gift, which shows that his higher qualities had won their trust. Yet his natural make-up seems more that of soldier than statesman—but a soldier who would never swerve from the path of duty no matter into what dangers it might lead him.

² FIRST HOUSES. Doubt exists as to whether the first settlers built in the neighborhood of Collins' Cove or in what is now the central part of Salem.

³ CONY AND HEDGEHOG. One stormy day, out of pity a cony let a hedgehog share her burrow. The hedgehog repaid the kindness by driving the poor cony cut of her own burrow with its sharp pricks.

⁴ THE PHYSICIAN was Samuel Fuller. He was also deacon of the Pilgrim Church.

⁵ THREE MINISTERS were Bright, Skelton and Higginson.

⁶ SALEM was so named (Peace) because of the peaceful settlement of disputes arising between old and new planters which had grown into a "dangerous jarre." The name is from Ps. lxxvi. 2.

⁷ FIRST CHURCH OF SALEM. The first fully organized Congregational Church in America, Aug. 1629. Samuel Skelton and Francis Higginson were pastor and teacher. The building, restored, stands in rear of Plummer Hall, Salem.

THE GREAT EMIGRATION, 1630.

HAVING settled Endicott in New England the Company at home next petitioned for a royal charter, which the king alone could give them. So far they were a company for colonization only. It would seem that the Puritans had resolved to found a free state in New England for among them were men of broad views. Charles I. granted them a very liberal charter in 1629. It changed them from a company of merchants into a political body with officers in lawful authority, and power to govern themselves almost independently. It created a legislature, or General Court,¹ with ability to do whatever might be found needful for maintaining or defending the colony in the enjoyment of its privileges. Though they had tried and tried again the Pilgrims could never obtain such a charter as this.

Directly the Company met in secret council to see whether they would remove the seat of government from London to New England, as some had proposed doing, or keep it in England where it was. The proposers reasoned that where the body was the head should also be. Moreover, they claimed that such re-

MASSACHUSETTS COLONY, 1630.

moval would free them from the annoying oversight of the king's ministers and bishops. In England their hands would be tied. In England they could never act quite freely or fearlessly. This was the only way in which they could work with free hands. Their best friends believed the colony could be made a success in no other way.

This step was agreed upon by general consent and the Company newly organized with John Winthrop[2] as governor, in the room of Matthew Cradock.

With great earnestness the company then set about getting ready ships to take out all who might wish to go to New England, for the number promised to be very great. Because throughout the length and breadth of the kingdom the Puritans were looking eagerly toward New England as their Promised Land. Though forbidden to meet together for public or private worship, and closely watched in every town and hamlet of the realm, they found ways of communicating with each other in spite of constables or pursuivants.[3] The times were every day growing darker and darker. The future looked even more gloomy. So widespread was this feeling of coming evil that when the Company called for emigrants near fifteen hundred persons came to the designated seaports.

Tracts setting forth the plans of the undertakers were scattered throughout England. The Company promised to give a piece of land to every colonist who should contribute money or goods to a common fund. He bought a share and became a shareholder. This land was to be his own. The money he paid went to equip and victual the ships, to pay the sailors' wages and provide supplies for the colony. On this plan every man could be a freeholder, instead of a sort of bond-servant, as the Pilgrims had been. Some poor people went as servants, and those who paid their own expenses had land assigned to them.

In March 1630 one company of colonists sailed for New England in the ship Mary and John. Before sailing, these people had formed themselves into a church and they brought their own ministers[4] along with them. In six weeks they arrived safely at Nantasket where their captain put them on shore much against their will, as they had meant to settle on Charles River, and thought he should have carried them there.

Seeing their lonely situation some of the old planters kindly lent them a boat in which a party of picked men, all well armed, went to look up a location. This party landed first at Charlestown, where they found a house and several wigwams, but saw only one Englishman, who gave them a boiled bass to eat. It was all he had. They then rowed on up the Charles until they found it growing narrow and shallow, when they went on shore and encamped on the beautiful plain where the United States Arsenal now stands. The woods around them were full of Indians of whom the explorers stood in great fear. But they soon made friends with them.

The explorers thought to make their settlement here, and so remained on the ground several days; but meantime their friends having found at Mat´ta´pan a location which they liked, the boat party was called back. From this landing the neighborhood was long known as Dorchester Fields. And because many of these people belonged in Dorchester, England, they called their settlement at Mattapan, Dorchester.[5] It was begun early in June, or some time before that at Boston was.

By April, eleven other ships were ready or nearly so. Four sailed in company from the Isle of Wight on the 8th, and got fairly to sea on the 10th. On this day they lost sight of England.

Mt. Desert was the first land made by the Arbella, which was the foremost ship of the fleet, and had the governor on board. Then, as she sailed along, the great White Hills rose cloud-like in the distance; then Agamenticus, which was the landmark they were seeking.

At the Isles of Shoals a ship was seen riding at anchor: at Cape Ann another; with many fishing shallops sailing to and fro, as the Arbella drew in toward the land.

It was now early June,

"And what is so rare as a day in June?"

All was bright and beautiful. Wild flowers decked the green shores, whose exquisite odors charmed the sea-worn emigrants' senses. Nature seemed welcoming them with fairest smiles.

SAILING FROM THE ISLE OF WIGHT.

At four in the morning of the 12th of June, 1630, being close to her port, the Arbella fired two guns. Shortly after she came to anchor near the Cape Ann shore. Most of the people hastened on shore, where they found plenty of ripe strawberries growing wild in the fields. In the afternoon Endicott came from Salem to pay Winthrop a visit, after which Winthrop and some of the principal men and women went back with Endicott to Salem, where they supped on a good venison pasty and good beer.

¹ GREAT AND GENERAL COURT created by the charter of 1629, was so distinguished from the ordinary courts held by the Governor and Assistants. Four "great, general, and solemn" assemblies were ordered to be held in each year (Hilary, Easter, Trinity and Michaelmas Terms) for electing officers, admitting freemen and making laws. The ancient title given to its legislature is still retained by Massachusetts.

² JOHN WINTHROP was unquestionably the greatest man that the Puritan movement to New England produced. His marked qualities were sagacity, prudence, energy without bluster and self-control without indifference. In every great public exigency we find Winthrop the master-spirit, eventually controlling or guiding events. His administration was never free from difficulties, seldom from dangers of no common sort, yet his sagacious policy brought the colony safely through them. It is doubtful if any other man than he could have crushed the Antinomian movement. Where Winthrop was narrow it was the fault of his age. He was the determined foe of every innovation in government or religion, as he and others had established them. He had strong class prejudices, believed only the higher class should rule and was charged with sometimes overstepping the limits of his authority. But in every sense of the word Winthrop was a man among men—a statesman, dexterous in diplomacy, patient under restraint, firm in adversity and in all things an incorruptible patriot.

³ PURSUIVANT, a State messenger.

⁴ MINISTERS John Maverick and John Warham.

⁵ DORCHESTER was first settled on the seaside from Old Harbor to Savin Hill, and on the plain between; now part of Boston.

THE SETTLERS AT CHARLESTOWN.

THE founders of this colony had meant to build one large, fortified town. For this purpose they brought ordnance and munitions of war in abundance. Not finding the situation of Salem to their liking the head men at once set about looking up a better.

Two parties went up Charles and Mystic rivers as far as boats could go; for it seems to have been their mind to settle upon one of these rivers.

The reason why they preferred an inland situation to one on the seacoast was because whenever England went to war they would run the risk of having their town destroyed should they build where large ships could approach it. Indeed, at this very time word was brought that the French were coming to destroy them.

They had about made up their minds in favor of the Charles River, on account of better grazing and farming lands to be had a few miles up. But after bringing their ships round to Charlestown so many people had

EARLIEST MAP OF BOSTON AND VICINITY. SUPPOSED DATE 1635.

fallen sick of ship-fever[1] that the project had to be given up.

So rather from necessity than choice the principal settlement was begun early in July at Charlestown,[2] though we hear of none who favored it as a permanent site for their city.

Although coming in midsummer, instead of midwinter, the experience of these colonists was hardly different from the Pilgrims'. Camp life in July was certainly no hardship as compared with camp life in December, yet the old fatality seemed waiting on the coming of every colony, without regard to season.

This peninsula was much too small to subsist all the colonists with their cattle. They found only one spring and that one on the beach where every tide covered it, so that no water could be had till the tide fell. Consequently those who had many cattle drove them up

CRADOCK HOUSE, CALLED THE OLD FORT, MEDFORD, MASS.

Charles River to the place that the Dorchester men had first chosen, which they called Watertown. Still another party went up to the head of the tide on the Mystic, chose a location near the great marshes, and named it Medford. Here, then, are three initial points.

All the people, at first, dwelt in tents, booths, or wigwams pitched on and around the Town Hill,[3] which made the settlement look more like a camp than a city.

Having their government ready organized, no time

was lost in putting it in operation. One of the first things done was to send for Morton and hold him prisoner.

Too many people were huddled together for health. The seeds of ship-fever spread rapidly among them. Water was scarce. Nourishing food could not be had. Summer heat spread the infection from tent to tent. Numbers died and some lay long unburied in their poor hovels for want of hands to dig their graves.

By reason of this dreadful visitation the governor called a solemn fast which was held on July 30. This day was also chosen as most fitting to form a church and it was done accordingly.

Fear and despondency drove many away. Nearly, or quite, a hundred went home in the same ships that brought them over. Others went to Piscataqua. But their going could not dismay the stout-hearted ones who bore up bravely under their many afflictions. Winthrop, the governor, wrote home that if all were to be done over again he would do no differently. Dudley, the bluff deputy-governor, wrote that those who were left thought themselves no worse off for those who had gone.

Still, bear up as bravely as they might, their condition was no less one of great hardship and peril from which only equal good fortune could rescue them. They had learned too late that shiploads of poor emigrants do not make a colony.

Their church was the open air. Beneath the shade of a spreading tree their pastor, Mr. Wilson, [4] preached to them on the Sabbath. "We here enjoy God and Jesus Christ. Is not that enough?" Winthrop asks of his absent wife.

While thus distressed, their solitary neighbor Blackstone visited them. He invited them to come over to Shawmut to live. Among other reasons he gave, Blackstone said there was a fine spring at Shawmut.

Seeing always before them the high three-peaked mount that stood in the centre of Shawmut the settlers had already begun calling it Trimountain.[5] It is probable that the governor and others soon went to see whether a general removal would be for the best.

---

[1] SHIP-FEVER, or scurvy, broke out at sea. The passage was long and detention on shipboard spread the disease.

[2] CHARLESTOWN is now a part of Boston.

[3] TOWN HILL rises directly from the public square, next Boston side.

[4] REV. JOHN WILSON was regarded as the spiritual father of the colony. When the schism in his church took place on account of Mrs. Hutchinson he was Winthrop's strongest ally.

[5] TRIMOUNTAIN, TRIMOUNT and TREMONT are all different forms of the same word.

BOSTON EXPLORED AND SETTLED.

FRONTING Charlestown, a green hill[1] rose up from the water's edge. Its sea-face was a steep gravel bluff, quite like the present harbor headlands. At the foot of this bluff the explorers landed. Going round the beach under it they found the hill nearly cut off from the rest of the peninsula by two coves, one on the seaside and one on the riverside, with a creek connecting them. Crossing over the low, wet ground between these coves, they began to mount the second and highest hill, which they had christened Trimountain. The Indian paths they followed led to the spring Blackstone told them of. While tasting its sweetness they saw, beyond them, on the harbor side, another pretty high hill. The men

who had seen service in the wars said that cannon
planted on the hill where they landed and on this one
would easily defend the place. They showed how these

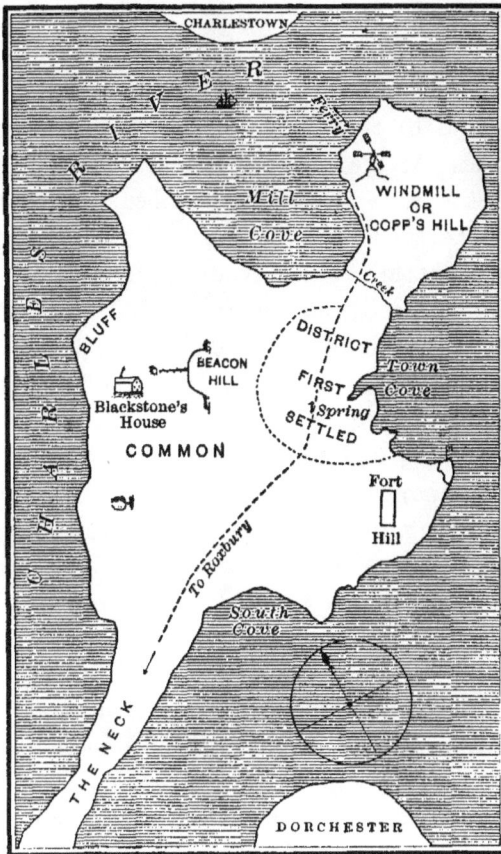

ORIGINAL FEATURES OF BOSTON.

two heights so protected the great cove as to make it a
safe harbor; while the one next Charlestown also would
defend the entrance to Charles River.

Shortly after passing the last or southernmost hill they came to a third cove. Three hills, the central one being highest, and three coves, the eastern being largest, were thus the prominent features of Trimountain.

When they had gone as far as they could, with the peninsula always growing narrower before them, the explorers came out of the woods at a point opposite the mainland to find that Trimountain was an island, at high tides. As the tide fell it laid bare a strip of sand and pebbles over which one could then pass to the mainland.[2] It was seen that the posting of a few men here would prevent any one invading them from the land side, quite as easily as fortifying the hills would keep out those who should approach from the sea. And, as we have said, the colonists looked first and foremost to making a good defence.

The explorers had to go through thickets, briars and swamps on their way in and out. They found a stagnant pool lying in a hollow of the great hill, not far from Blackstone's cottage; and near by a solitary native elm[3] was thriftily growing. All the ground was overgrown with huckleberry bushes. Beginning at this place, there was a goodly breadth of nearly level, or gently sloping, land all the way down to the seaside cove. It was high, dry and sunny and was the best for building, planting and pasturage.

Clumps of trees grew here and there; but the peninsula was nowhere thickly wooded, though there were many hollows and swampy places well covered with trees. Nor was there so much as a ledge to be seen. There were no Indians. Blackstone lived entirely alone.

Isaac Johnson was the richest man among the colonists and much looked up to by them. He favored a removal and was among the first to make the change of residence which soon became general.

So taking their tents and their flocks, like the Israelites of old, numbers crossed the river to Trimountain before the end of August.

In the first boatload that went over was a romping English girl named Anne Pollard, who lived to be over a hundred years old. As the boat drew near the shore she laughingly said that she would be the first one to land, and getting on the bow she jumped to the strand before any one else. In doing this she had only repeated what Mary Chilton did at Plymouth, ten years before her. Leaving behind them the height next Charlestown, all took their way to the vicinity of the great cove and spring. The path trod by these people in going to and fro thus became the very first highway on Trimountain.

While this was going on, the chief men continued for a while longer to transact the public business at Charlestown. But so many had crossed the river to stay that on the 7th of September by their style, which would now be reckoned the 17th by ours, they held a court at which it was ordered that Trimountain should be called Boston.[4] This was the name they had all along meant to give their first town.

---

[1] CONSULT plan, p. 165.

[2] ORIGINAL CONDITION of Washington Street above Dover.

[3] THE ELM was doubtless the same as that so long known as the Great Elm, which was blown down in 1876.

[4] BOSTON was named for Boston in Lincolnshire, Eng. The name itself is supposed to be a corruption of that of St. Botolph a Saxon saint who lived in the early part of the Christian era. Many of the colonists were from Lincolnshire and some of their most influential patrons lived there. No better reason can be given for the adoption of the name.

THE PILGRIMS OF BOSTON.

THE Boston settlers located themselves chiefly around the great cove. Isaac Johnson took the square now enclosed by Washington, Court, Tremont and School streets. Governor Winthrop chose a spot nearest the

LANDMARK IN SETTLED DISTRICT.

J, First burial place. W, Winthrop's house. S, The spring gate (Spring Lane). M, Market-place. C, The first church. P, Rev. Mr. Wilson's house. M. R., Original water front (Merchants' Row).

spring. People who came from the same towns in England formed little neighborhoods. Their cattle were turned out to get their own living.

Hardly had a beginning been made when Mr. Johnson died. His death was much deplored for he was a wise and pious man whose whole heart was set upon the success of the colony. He was buried in a corner of his own lot, which in this way became Boston's first burial place.[1]

The people saw that the great cove was to be their harbor, so they named it the Town Cove. They decided to have a beacon on the highest hill, a fort on the southernmost, and a mill on that next Charlestown. Very soon Bostonians spoke of their three eminences as Windmill Hill, Beacon Hill, and Fort Hill.

Near the centre of settlement they laid out a marketplace. On one side they by and by built a little church with mud walls and thatched roof; and on the other a house for Rev. John Wilson, their minister.

But before this was done William Pynchon with others had settled Roxbury (Sept. 28).

FIRST CHURCH OF BOSTON.

So that by the time Boston was fairly begun a chain of settlements stretched round it on the mainland. Very small and feeble ones they were. With these added the whole now numbered ten[2] in Massachusetts.

The plantation at Watertown was begun by Sir Richard Saltonstall[3] and his followers. That at Medford was begun by Matthew Cradock's agent, with men and cattle sent over for the purpose. When it was thought best to separate, the leading men took charge of little communities of their own friends or servants.

Very busy were these September days in all the plantations. At Boston all their household goods, provisions and animals had to be brought across the river. The time spent at Charlestown was as good as wasted.

COMMUNION VESSEL.

Every thing had to be done over again with autumn close at hand. The planting season was over. Instead of getting fresh provisions at Salem to recruit their sick, they had found many of the people there destitute and begging for help for themselves. Winthrop had the wise foresight to hasten one of the ships home for a supply of food: and it was well that he did so.

Some houses, however, were got ready for the winter. They were roughly built, thatched cottages with wooden chimneys plastered with clay. No time could be wasted on show. Each completed house sheltered as many as it would hold, but the greater number continued to live in tents or wigwams for want of means to build for themselves. And these poor people fared badly.

So far the settlers had battled with disease, but not with want. Their letters say "Though we have not beef and mutton yet, God be praised! we want them not. Our Indian corn answers for all. Yet here is fowl and fish in great plenty."

WINTHROP'S FLAGON.

So touching the country, they told their friends that they saw little difference between the country and England. There was as good land but none so poor: sweet air, fair rivers, plenty of springs, with better water than in England. No want of any thing to those who brought means "to raise out of the earth or sea." In a word the knee-timber of the enterprise was money.

Wolves prowled round the plantations. Goats and swine were killed every day. In October the settlers began to be pinched by scarcity. Maverick then went with some of them to Narragansett to buy corn. Once a day, at low tide, the women would go and gather clams and mussels on the shore. Ground-nuts and acorns supported them as they had Weston's starving men. By the end of October their provisions were almost exhausted and famine threatened them nearly. One man walked to Plymouth and back to get a little corn for his family. Another has

CHOPPING-KNIFE.

told how he longed for the crusts he used to see on his father's table. Some had their last loaf in the oven, some had nothing left.

Fortune showed them favor in one way. The winter was mild and open with only light frosts till the end of December. Bitter cold then set in. The rivers quickly froze up. Snow covered the ground. The poor beasts could no longer get their own living abroad but wandered up and down without shelter or food. Those who dwelt in tents became sickly and many died. More must have perished from want but for the timely arrival of the expected ship. For this relief a thanksgiving was ordered to be held instead of the fast that had already been appointed, to seek God in their afflictions.

¹ FOR DETAILS concerning the topography or landmarks consult "Old Landmarks of Boston." See plan, p. 168.

² TEN SETTLEMENTS, Winnisimmet, Wessagusset, Salem, Charlestown, Dorcheater, Boston, Watertown, Roxbury, Medford, Nantasket.

³ SIR RICHARD SALTONSTALL is the only titled personage who came to New England with these emigrante. He was one of the Assistants. He went back to England the next year, after settling Watertown, and did not again return.

THE HEART OF THE COMMONWEALTH.

THE Boston of 1631 was a place of so much misery and destitution that it was often spoken of as "Lost-Town."

Things, however, began to mend, though owing to the bad reports carried home by those who had deserted

SUN-DIAL, WHEEL AND CHAIR.

the settlements, not a hundred people came over the second year. Regard was had to public safety by order ing all able-bodied men to keep arms, and by forming them into train-bands. A watchful eye was kept on the Indians in whom the settlers did not put great trust. Moreover, before the summer was over, the Tarratines made one of their raids upon the Agawams, many of whom were killed and wounded. The Agawams fled for protection to the English, thus throwing them into alarm for their own safety. So the colonists had good cause to be always on the alert.

Chic'a'tau'but, the aged sachem of Neponset, presently paid the governor a visit of ceremony. Though now having little power, he came in state with many in his train. The governor made a feast, for the others, but took the chief to his own house, where Chicataubut behaved with great propriety.

Also a band of Connecticut River Indians came all the way to Boston to entreat for help to defend their country against the Pequots. They offered lands and gifts if the English would go and live among them. In this way, most of the colonists now heard for the first time of the Connecticut.

As a rule these colonists were wealthier than the Pilgrims. Consequently they had more comforts. Otherwise there was little difference in houses, garb or way of living, between them. Each was jealous of the other, though

HANGING-LAMP.

by and by mutual interest brought them to act together.

Their early dispersion among many places troubled the Massachusetts colonists. They had meant to follow the Pilgrims' example; live all together in one strong, well-built town. It led to divided counsels and for a while it checked Boston's growth.

In the time of doubt and misgiving the chief men had agreed to carry out their first plan, and begin a new town in the spring. It was to be on the Charles, and was meant for the capital. Accordingly, some of them

did go to the place agreed upon, but it was found that the Boston people, most of whom had once before removed, would not do so again. So the plan for a general removal fell to the ground, though most of those who had gone already kept their purpose, and called their settlement Newtown. This was the way Cambridge came to be settled, for Cambridge was first called Newtown.

The next year (1632) Boston was fixed upon as being the best place for public meetings.

While ploughing, planting and building kept the settlers employed, the rulers found work to do in allotting lands, making orders or punishing the idle and vicious. Morton, with some others, had been sent away to England, and now Walford, the original settler at Charlestown, was also banished for his contempt of authority.

IN THE STOCKS.

For swearing, drunkenness or theft, the offender was tied up to a post and received a certain number of lashes from the beadle's whip. No one could settle among them or go outside the colony without leave obtained of the authorities. Sober and orderly conduct was strictly enforced. The lawbreaker and the vicious person were equally certain of punishment, since it was meant to have a government both of law and morals.

Besides banishment, whipping, and imprisonment, in the Puritan colony branding with a hot iron, and slitting, or boring, the ears were sometimes inflicted. Sitting in the stocks or bilboes or standing in the pillory were common penalties for minor offences. Sometimes a criminal was made to wear a large capital letter[1] sewed on the outer garment, and so to carry the sign of disgrace about with him. The colonists had to build a prison before they did a schoolhouse.

IN THE BILBOES.

Going from crimes to what are called sumptuary laws, the rulers ordered every one who had cards or dice to destroy them. They forbade the use of tobacco. They did away with the ancient custom of drinking to each other at meals; also the wearing of long hair by men and veils by women. One was thought a vain, the other an im-

PILLORY.

modest practice. For the same reason display in dress was reproved by forbidding the wearing of lace, points, ruffs or slashed sleeves. And in this respect the rulers set the example of economy and simplicity for the rest.

Wisely or not, the Puritan colonists now decided that none but members of their own church should be made freemen of the colony. By their charter only freemen were allowed to vote or hold office. Unless, therefore, he were a member of one of the churches, a colonist could have no share in public affairs. He was a citizen without political rights, or as we should now say an alien. And, as only Puritan churches[2] were permitted, the colonists had set up a Puritan State of which the church was the corner stone.

It was in the meeting-house that the people came together both to worship and transact public business. The minister was supported by a tax laid on all citizens alike. He held a public station of high trust. Church and State being one, he preached on all questions of public concern, and as the people had made the Bible their code of laws they looked most to him for instruction. So really the church gave direction to public affairs because public opinion was mostly formed by it. And so each church was not only a legal, inseparable part of each community, but its unit of force.

This close union of Church and State was a grievance to many who could not, or would not, join the Puritan congregations. They complained of it as establishing a tyranny, similar in all respects to that which the Puritans had declared

WEATHER-VANE.

they could not live under. But the Puritans were firmly resolved not to open the door to those whom they considered adversaries. So the line was strictly drawn between them and the others, and as strictly maintained.

Although that form of government in which only part of the people had a voice could not be called a popular government, yet the seed of a democracy was sown in thus forming church-members into a body politic, because it brought the common people to take an active part in the public business.

Union in church fellowship led the people commonly to address each other as "brother" and "sister." But the class distinctions of old England were long observed. A mechanic, farmer or laborer was always spoken of as Goodman so and so. No one belonging to these callings could be a "Gentleman"[3] as that title was given only to those standing between the nobility and working-class. We learn how highly it was esteemed from the fact that a man who had been convicted of theft was condemned thereafter to be called plain Josias, instead of Mr. Josias Plaistow, as he had been formerly.

Besides the servants, or apprentices, Samuel Maverick had a few negro slaves. But it was yet some time before blacks were bought or sold like other property. After a time owning slaves became a common practice with all who could afford it.

GENTLEMAN IN RUFF.

After the second year multitudes flocked to the colony. So many came over that the king became alarmed and tried to put a stop to it. Many were people of means. All wanted land, for all were farmers. Indeed, the new-comers were so numerous that Boston was not three years old before the people everywhere complained of being too much crowded.

At this time they heard with real alarm that the

French had not only seized upon the Pilgrims' trading-house at Penobscot,[4] but had threatened to expel the English all along the coast. When asked to show his authority for this act the French officer had touched his sword-hilt and said, "This is my commission."

Taking alarm at this menace the Massachusetts rulers made haste to send off a dozen men to secure possession of Agawam before any intruders should do so. Governor Winthrop's son John led the party. This was in March, 1633. The next year Agawam was made a town by the name of Ipswich,[5] and for the present it continued to be the frontier town of the colony, or in a military sense, an advanced post toward the enemy to prevent surprise.

CAVALIER.

Besides offering a good defence, with access by the river from the sea, and Salem within supporting distance, it will be remembered that Agawam was the seat of the tribe which gave the place its earliest name. The English believed that the French would urge on the Tarratines, their allies, to renewed acts of hostility, and as the Agawams were friendly, they felt that by giving them support they would also be defending themselves. But they dared not go farther into the wilderness at this time.

The men who first settled Ipswich gave it a prestige that soon drew others of like quality to join them.

The place itself had been over-praised by Smith who reasoned that where the Indians located their chief villages, would be found the choicest lands. This was partly true. But Indians were often governed by reasons which did not apply to the white man's wants. They however welcomed the English among them as their defenders, sold them lands, and as friends and neighbors helped them to get settled.

There was much open meadow, and the Indians had cleared a good breadth of upland for planting when they were a more numerous people. A chain of low hills stretched along the seacoast in front. Creeks and water courses ran through the intervening marshes. On the east the country was also open. With these natural safeguards the small band of Englishmen felt quite secure. But as the risk was great only a few were allowed to go in the first place.

[1] CAPITAL LETTER. "D" for drunkard, "A" for adulterer, etc. The motive of Hawthorne's "Scarlet Letter."

[2] PURITAN CHURCHES. Smarting under the memory of recent persecution the Puritans became in their turn persecutors of the church that had persecuted them. They also believed that if Episcopal Churches were allowed, bishops would be sent over to govern them and a hierarchy created with all the evils from which they had fled. Moreover the Pilgrims had set them the example of excluding non-church-members from a share in the government.

[3] A GENTLEMAN by their law could not be whipped.

[4] PENOBSCOT TAKEN. The unequal struggle between France and England over the Huguenots had ended with the taking of La Rochelle. Then came the treaty of St. Germain by which Acadia was restored to France, but leaving the old French claim to New England unsettled. While engaged in war at home, Cardinal Richelieu—The Great Cardinal —had conceived the idea of putting new life into the affairs of Canada and at the same time checking the English. A new company was formed of which Richelieu was the head. In most things it was patterned after the Dutch East India Company. No foreigner or heretic was to be admitted into the colony. Under the vigorous policy inaugurated by Richelieu the move to recover Acadia was begun at Penobscot.

[5] IPSWICH. From Ipswich, Suffolk Co., Eng. The first minister was Rev. Nathaniel, or Nat, Ward, who wrote a witty, though not very favorable, account of the country entitled the "Simple Cobbler of Agawam." He went back to England.

TOWN AND COLONY.

LITTLE has been said about the government of the colony or its workings. In the first place the charter stood for a constitution. Indeed, it was a written constitution, for in it the whole frame of government was ready fitted to be put together when the colonists got to New England.

All they had to do was to come together at stated times in order to elect officers, make laws or consider such other public business as might come before them. Their body was called The Great and General Court.

Once a year they chose a governor, deputy-governor and eighteen of their ablest men to act as helps to the governor. Therefore these eighteen counsellors were called Assistants.

The Governor and Assistants formed a lesser court whose duties were to execute the laws, with power to do certain other things which the charter named. We should now call it the executive power.

COLONY SEAL.

At first the colonial authorities took charge of every thing. But presently town governments were formed on the model of the colonial. So simple, yet so perfect, is this model that the American village has often been called the germ of states and empires.

All the citizens met and chose a certain number of their principal men to whom the town's affairs were to be intrusted. These overseers were afterward called Selectmen.[1] When the inhabitants came together about the town's business it was called a Town-Meeting.[2] They first chose a Moderator who put questions to vote and kept order.

The Boston settlers cut off the Neck with a fence, in which was a gate and stile, for travellers who, in going to and fro, made a footway through the peninsula. In time the footpath grew to be a cartway which, in the settled part of the town, was called The Street.

Blackstone soon left them. Though he had invited the settlers to come there, it is said that he did not like their company when they had come. So rather than stay he went to Rehoboth,[3] which was then a wilderness.

The settlers had given him a home-lot of fifty acres, near his house. They had also made him a freeman. But Blackstone was an Episcopalian and he could not join their church. It is also evident that he wished to live alone.

He therefore sold most of his land to the town for thirty pounds, or about a hundred and fifty dollars of our money. The town then set apart the tract to be kept as a pasture and training-field for the common use of all the inhabitants. And this was the origin of the noble park situated in the heart of Boston. It was originally a Common, not only in name, but in the uses to which it was put.

Philemon Pormont was the first schoolmaster. John Coggan opened the first shop and Samuel Cole the first inn. Market days were established. Swine were not allowed to run at large. More orderly building was looked to, as the first comers had mostly built along the crooked paths, to which crooked streets and lanes were the successors.

Stirring events were at hand. The new colony was destined to grow up with strife within and without. First the colonists heard that the Pequots had killed some English traders. They were next alarmed by the report that Endicott had cut out the cross from the national ensign, because the cross in it was a symbol of the Roman Church. Most people were offended, for they revered their country's flag. The timid ones dreaded the King's anger. So Endicott was censured for his hasty act.

CUTTING OUT THE CROSS.

Increase of population made the coming together of all the freemen in General Court, which was the old way, no longer feasible. The more the colony spread out the greater the hardship became. It was therefore settled that in future each town should send deputies instead. This was the beginning of representative government[4] in Massachusetts.

When these deputies met for the annual election, all had to pass through a room where the Governor and Assistants sat in state. Each deputy dropped his paper ballot into a hat and then went out. Elections were sometimes hotly contested, and canvassing for votes went on in much the same way that it does to-day. It is said that at one election Rev. Mr. Wilson climbed a tree, the better to make a speech to the voters.

Indeed, the clergy took a prominent part in all matters of public concern. Both in the pulpit and out they had great influence. No ceremony was thought to be complete without the minister. No matter was undertaken without consulting him. So at the election of 1634 the Rev. Mr. Cotton preached to the deputies. After this it grew into a custom to have a sermon on Election Day which, consequently, was called The Election Sermon.

On the Sabbath morn the loud drum called the settlers to church. Those who did not go were fined. There being no printing-presses as yet, when a proclamation had to be made public a trumpeter [5] was sent abroad from town to town on horseback. When he rode into a village he would wind his horn loudly, whereupon the people would gather round him to hear the news.

Meanwhile, hardy settlers had pushed out as far as Newbury [6] on the north, Hingham [7] on the south, and Concord [8] on the west. Some, more adventurous still, had gone prospecting as far even as the Connecticut: and these were loud in praise of that beautiful river.

By the settlement of Newbury the frontier was advanced as far as the banks of the Merrimack, with the space of a few leagues only separating it from the Piscataqua, or New Hampshire, settlements. This fine stream, so strangely overlooked by the first explorers of our coasts, would have opened up to them, had they but known it, a practicable way into the interior. They had missed it and it remained for years neglected.

The original settlers of Newbury went from Ipswich. They are supposed to have gone by water, ascending Parker River, which was so named for Rev. Thomas

Parker, one of their party and their first minister. Very soon after, a second plantation was begun on the opposite bank of the Merrimack, at its mouth. This was named Salisbury. Then a third, called Rowley, filled the wide gap between Ipswich and Newbury, thus closing up the coast line of settlements extending between Plymouth Colony and the province of New Hampshire.

[1] SELECTMEN. The same body exists to-day, because experience has shown it to be the best for small communities.

[2] TOWN-MEETING. John Adams enumerates town-meetings, training-days, town-schools and ministers as prime elements of a free commonwealth.

[3] REHOBOTH (Hebrew) originally included Seekonk, Mass., and Pawtucket and Cumberland, R.I., Seekonk being the Indian name for them all. Blackstone's actual place of residence was "Study Hill," in Cumberland, R.I. Hence he was the first white inhabitant of that State. Blackstone River, on the east side of which he settled, and the town of Blackstone, Mass., perpetuate his memory and traces of his well and grave are yet remaining.

[4] REPRESENTATIVE GOVERNMENT continued in one body until a dispute arose about a stray pig. A woman prosecuted a citizen for stealing and killing her pig. The case finally went to the General Court where the hearing occupied seven days. On a final vote a majority of the Assistants were for acquittal and a majority of Deputies for conviction, but as no sentence could pass without having a majority of both Assistants and Deputies the action failed. This virtual control of the General Court by the minority bred a jealousy which led to separating it into two bodies.

[5] TRUMPETER, a sort of herald and relic of the days of chivalry. An officer to whom the Town Crier succeeded.

[6] OLD NEWBURY was the first settled. Newburyport is of later origin. The choice was determined by the meadow lands rather than prospective commercial advantage, as the settlers were farmers. For their purpose they chose with judgment. But in time they found the Merrimack their truest source of greatness. Read with this Whittier's "Prophecy of Samuel Sewall."

[7] HINGHAM, originally Bear's Cove.

[8] CONCORD (Indian Musketaquid). The first settlers lived in rude huts and caves on the hillside between the Public Square and Merriam's Corner. Their first winter was one of much misery.

INDIAN CHARACTER.

INSIGHT. Edward Winslow, of Plymouth, was a great favorite of King Massasoit's. Once, when Winslow came to the king's lodge, after a journey, Massasoit offered to go to Plymouth with him. But before they set out, the king privately sent one of his men on before to spread the report that Winslow was dead. the messenger did as he was bid, and there was great sorrow among the Pilgrims. The very next day Massasoit brought Winslow safe home. When asked why this false report had been sent, Massasoit answered

SAMP PAN.

that it was the Indians' way of making an absent friend's welcome more joyful.

JUSTICE. The Indians were very eager to find out how to make gunpowder. A white trader who sold some to an Indian, told him to sow it in the ground, and it would grow like wheat. The Indian was greatly elated. He went home and sowed some of his powder without delay. Month after month he watched for it to

MOCCASON.

sprout, and winter came before he found out the cheat that had been put upon him. He said nothing, but some time after, when the trader had forgotten all about his practical joke, the Indian bought a lot of goods of him, on credit. When the time came, the trader went to the Indian and demanded payment. The Indian quietly heard him through, then looking him in the eye, said, "Me pay you when my powder grow."

SENSITIVENESS. An Indian of the Kennebec tribe who had done good service in the wars, received from the whites a grant of land and settled among them. Though not ill-treated, yet the common prejudice against Indians prevented any sympathy with him. This was shown at the death of his only child when none of his neighbors came near him. Shortly after he went to some of them, and said with feeling, "When white man's child die, Indian sorry. He help bury him. When my child die, no one speak to me. I make his grave alone. I can no live here." He gave up his home, dug up the body of his child, and carried it two hundred miles to Canada.

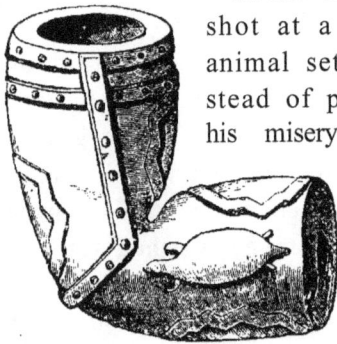

M IND IN A NIMAL S. A hunter once shot at a bear and wounded it. The animal set up a most piteous cry. Instead of putting the poor beast out of his misery the Indian went to where he lay groaning and spoke to him as follows: "Harkye bear! You are a coward and no warrior as you pretend to be. Were you a warrior you would show it by your firmness, and not cry and whimper like an old woman. You know, bear, that our tribes are at war with each other. You have found the Indians too strong for you and you have gone sneaking about the woods, stealing their hogs. Perhaps you have hog's flesh in your belly now. Had you conquered me, I would have borne it with courage, and have died like a brave warrior, but you, bear, sit here and cry, and disgrace your tribe by your cowardice." He then despatched him. When asked how he thought the bear could understand him, he replied, "Oh! bear understand me very well. Did you no see how 'shamed he looked?"

CLAY PIPE WITH TURTLE TOTEM.

V.

OUTSWARMS FROM THE MOTHER COLONY.

THE PIONEERS OF CONNECTICUT, 1635.

HITHERTO the Dutch at New Amsterdam had nearly monopolized the Indian trade throughout Long Island Sound. They had forestalled the English in Narragansett Bay, in the Pequot, and in the Connecticut Rivers. While enjoying this exclusive privilege of trade, they made no effort to take formal possession anywhere, but so soon as they saw that the Pilgrims were minded to do this the Dutch suddenly resolved to be beforehand with them.

To this end they sent out men who made a fort which they named "Good Hope"[1] at Suckiag (Hartford) in the summer of 1633.

The Pilgrims also had got ready a bark, with the frame of a house on board, ready to be put up without loss of time. When they came to the fort the Dutch asked them where they were going. The Pilgrims answered, "We are going up the river to trade." The Dutch then ordered them to stop or they would fire into them. Then the Pilgrims bade them fire away for stop they would not.

So the bold Pilgrims sailed past the fort without further hinderance. They landed their goods and set up their trading-house on the site of Windsor, so cutting off the Dutch from the upper river. The Dutch, indeed,

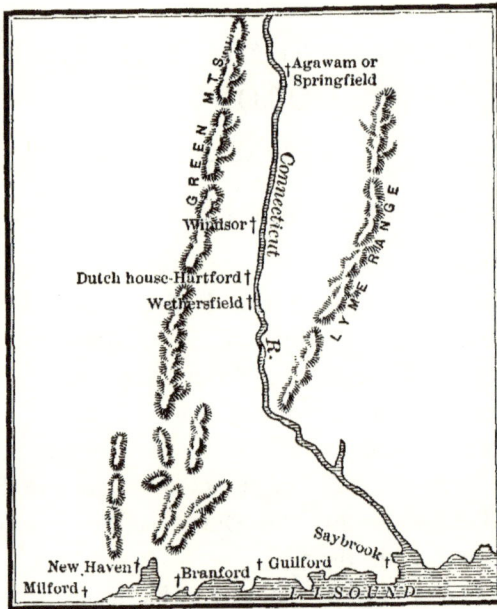

CONNECTICUT AND NEW HAVEN COLONIES.

brought a company of soldiers to drive them away, but on seeing that the Plymouth men would not yield without a fight, the wrathful Hollanders went back as they came.

This happened in the autumn of 1633. The next winter is memorable for the dreadful havoc that the small-pox made among the Indians. Again, as of old,

they died off by scores and hundreds. The Narragansetts alone lost seven hundred men. Other tribes suffered in like proportion. Hearing what numbers had
been swept away, the people around Boston thought it
opened the door for their proposed removal.

We have told how an Indian embassy came to solicit
an alliance with the Bostonians. They offered to hold

ANCIENT MEETING-HOUSE.

their country as vassals of the English. Meantime the
fierce Pequots had subdued those Indians and overrun
their country. Crafty and cruel, the Pequots had killed
both English and Dutch traders. The Dutch retaliated
by killing some of the Pequots. The powerful Narragansetts were hereditary enemies of the Pequots. Now,
though their great Sachem Canonicus had once sent a

defiance to the Pilgrims, the Narragansetts had after kept on good terms with the English. But as for the Pequots, the Narragansetts stood ready to fight them whenever they could do so to advantage.

So the cunning Pequots having the always hostile Narragansetts on one side, and seeing the Dutch as ready to take revenge on the other, in their turn sought the alliance of the Bostonians. Their runner brought two bundles of sticks to signify how many skins and how much wampum his nation would give to have peace. The Pequots also promised to submit themselves to the English, and wished them to come to Connecticut. So a peace was concluded.

The way being thus opened, small parties of settlers soon set out for Connecticut, going both by land and water.[2] With great toil and fatigue, these people made their way through swamps and thickets, where no white man had yet ventured before them.

Common report said that the Connecticut took its rise so near the great northern lake that the Indians crossed over from one to the other in a day's march. Great account was made of the beaver which it was thought might be turned away from the Dutch by settling on this river. But the chief reason why so many English wished to go to the Connecticut was because of the fertile meadow lands there, of which they had heard.

A large emigration took place in 1635, of people from Watertown, Newtown (Cambridge) and Dorchester. Their removal was strongly opposed on the ground that it would weaken the colony. But two entire churches, with their ministers, had resolved to go. Their going was quaintly likened to the removal of two candlesticks set in the dark wilderness.

The Watertown people settled what is now Wethers-field,[3] the Newtown people went to Hartford, and those from Dorchester to Windsor, though these places at first had other names.

Both the Dutch and the Pilgrims felt aggrieved at this intrusion of the Massachusetts people, but stay it they could not, as the growing power of the emigrants soon made them the masters.

In the same year another important settlement was made. This one was planned in England and had nothing to do with the upper settlements.

The younger John Winthrop had rendered essential aid to the Governor, his father, in setting forth the Massachusetts Colony. He had staid in England until the next year (1631) when he followed his father to New England. The plantation at Ipswich was begun by him. He soon went back to England, at which time the Lords Say and Brook, and other noble persons, gave him commission to begin a plantation for them at the mouth of the Connecticut. For this purpose they sent men, money and an able engineer named Lion Gardiner.[4]

Late in the autumn (November) Winthrop sent twenty men to take possession.

Knowing that if a fort were built here it would shut them out of the river, the Dutch tried to seize upon the same place. They failed because the English had al-ready got some guns on shore and would not let the Dutchmen land. So the English were now masters of the river. This plantation was afterward called Say-brook [5] in compliment to its two noble patrons.

The Dutch at Good Hope being in this manner "bottled up," the Pilgrims in their turn had to make the most of a bad bargain. Their complaints were rather coldly treated, but at length a compromise was made with those who had intruded upon their lands.

As for the Hollanders, the differences between them and the English being referred to the home governments the English minister at The Hague advised the colonists "to keep on crowding the Dutch."

[1] GOOD HOPE. The Dutch trading-post was situated on the point of land where Mill River joins the Connecticut. The Indian title was purchased of the Pequots after their conquest of the river region. But having located themselves within the New England Charter limits the Dutch were regarded by the English as intruders and were so treated. They however held possession of Good Hope until 1653 when their house was seized au the property of aliens.

[2] OLDHAN went overland in the summer of 1633. A trading-bark was also sent from Boston to the river. Under the date of Jan. 1 Winthrop mentions that "Hall and the two others who went to Connecticut in November came now home, having lost themselves and endured much misery."

[3] WETHERSFIELD (Indian Pequag). The English first called it Watertown.

[4] LION GARDINER became proprietor of the fertile island at the east end of Long Island which bears his name, as Gardiner's Bay also does.

[5] SAYBROOK PATENT could hardly be definitely located by its given boundaries, which were from Narragansett River forty leagues (a hundred and twenty miles) upon a straight line near the sea-shore, toward the southwest as the coast ran. It however stopped the Dutch from encroaching further upon New England territory which the Council for New England had often been entreated to prevent. Besides the two noblemen, Lord Say and Lord Brook, whose names Saybrook perpetuates, the two great commoners Hampden and Pym were among the patentees and it is more than probable that they as well as Cromwell meditated, if they did not actually attempt, a removal to New England. Read English history of this period.

PIONEERS OF CONNECTICUT—*Continued.*

THOSE people who had first begun plantations did not escape hardship or suffering. Many went back in the late autumn to their old homes in order to avoid starvation in the new.

When spring came, nearly all who were left at Newtown followed their friends to Hartford. They drove their flocks before them, and lived on their milk by the way.

Their pastor, Thomas Hooker,[1] travelled with them, his invalid wife being borne in a horse-litter.

Other dissatisfied colonists soon followed the example of these pioneers. In 1636 William Pynchon led a party from Roxbury to the great meadows situated above Windsor, then known by the Indian name of Agawam. They settled here, and later (1640) it was called Spring-field.[2]

WILLIAM PYNCHON.

All these river settlements, except Saybrook, at first consented to be under the authority of Massachusetts, though they soon (1638, old style) formed a little confederacy, under written articles of agreement, of their own. But not until 1662 did they obtain a royal charter giving them powers of government, and defining their boundaries.

John Haynes[3] was one of the framers of their first compact, and he was chosen their first governor under it.

They took the name of Connecticut Colony from the great river, while Massachusetts had begun to be familiarly designated as the Bay Colony, and the long wilderness way between as the Bay Path.[4]

Having wisely made their settlements close together these colonists could give each other a helping hand in time of need, and the need came quickly.

[1] THOMAS HOOKER, an English Puritan divine, after much persecution came in 1633 to New England. He was at once settled over the church at Newtown which followed him to Connecticut in a body. This fact, taken with others, shows what hold Hooker had upon his people who seemed to have look to

him as their Moses. It is not unlikely that this removal may be attributed in some part to jealousy which the bringing together in a narrow field of so many eminent men naturally created. Late comers, like Hooker, found the higher places in Church and Commonwealth already filled.

² SPRINGFIELD was so named in honor of its founder's English residence. Its settlers had leave to go under like conditions with other emigrants to Connecticut. They built their first house on the west side of the river, in the meadow since called House-Meadow, but subsequently went to the other side on finding that the low lands were subject to overflow. An agreement was entered into providing for the settlement of a minister, division of lands, with limitation of their whole number to fifty families, and raising means to defray public charges.

³ JOHN HAYNES came with Hooker to Boston. His abilities advanced him first to the place of Assistant and next (1635) to that of Governor of Massachusetts. All accounts concede him great personal worth as well as capacity for public station. He was most influential and persevering in pushing on the movement to Connecticut, where his administration was wise and memorable.

⁴ THE BAY PATH followed nearly the same route as the present great high-road leading from Boston to Springfield via Brookfield. It was marked by "blazed" trees (trees from which the bark is chipped) and instead of villages there were certain camping-places at the end of each day's march which in time became populous towns. But the first travellers often lost themselves. J. G. Holland has written a romance of the early days entitled the "Bay Path," with Springfield for its scene of action.

RHODE ISLAND AND PROVIDENCE PLANTATIONS, 1636–1637.

ROGER WILLIAMS,¹ the founder of Rhode Island, came to New England in 1631. He was one of those Puritan ministers who sought a refuge from persecution. He was at first minister at Salem, then at Plymouth and then at Salem again, though he did not stay long in either place. Men of his own time say that Williams was a "godly and zealous" man, but one of "very unsettled judgment." One writer says he had a "windmill in his head."

Williams thought the rulers had laid down false principles of government. He therefore attacked those principles. The rulers thought Williams bent on sowing dangerous ideas which could only breed dissensions.

So they tried to stop his preaching them, first by mild then by harsh means, but at all events to stop them.

But Williams was fearless for the right, as he believed it. So he kept on until the Puritan fathers silenced him as the English bishops had silenced the Puritan ministers.

Meantime Williams had made some converts to his way of thinking, and most people admired him, for he was a man of learning and ability. His own church at Salem held to him last and longest, but at length that too sorrowfully gave him up as a sheep that has strayed from the fold.

Roger Williams In maintained that all laws which fettered a man's conscience were unjust. Making it an offence to stay away from meeting was one. And if one was wrong then all were. He declared those things to lie between a man and his Maker. He censured the magistrates. He charged them with injustice and oppression, and the churches with corruption. In some things Williams was himself narrow, but in his

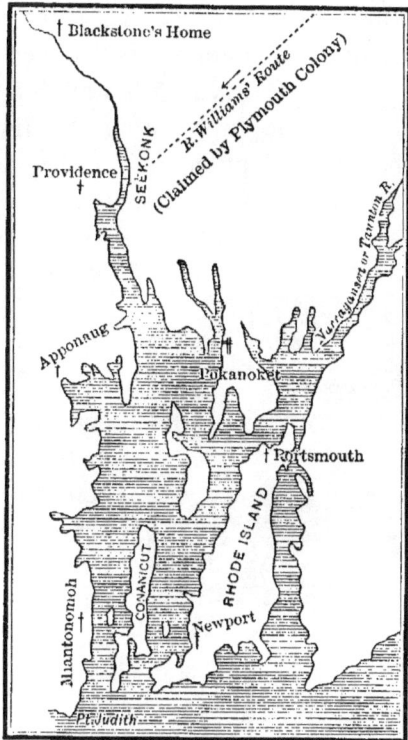

EARLY SETTLEMENTS IN RHODE ISLAND.

grand idea of religious tolerance he stood far ahead of his time.

Williams' aims were pure and noble. So was his character. But the Puritans had only just established their system and would by no means admit the need of such sweeping reform as he advocated. As Williams stoutly maintained his charges they banished him.

Both at Plymouth and Salem Williams had spent much time in learning the Indian tongue. To do this he often slept in their filthy, smoky holes, not thinking then of the great benefit it was to be to him by and by.

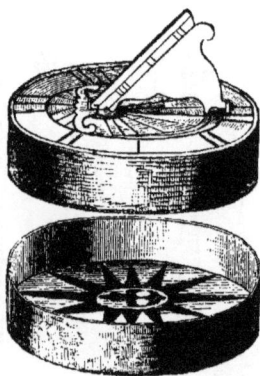

WILLIAMS' COMPASS AND DIAL.

Williams was allowed some stay of the sentence of exile, but he was commanded not to preach. Hearing that he was holding religious meetings at his house, officers were sent to take him into custody. Williams had timely notice of their coming from Governor Winthrop, who privately wrote him "to steer his course" for Narragansett Bay and the Indians.

Narragansett Bay was the great granary of early New England. The west shore and islands belonged to the Narragansetts. The east shore was the country of Massasoit. From the day of Verrazano's visit no white man had inhabited it. The Dutch and the Pilgrims had commerce with the natives but held no spot of ground on the shores of this great bay.

It was in the heart of winter. Leaving his wife and children behind, Roger Williams fled in secrecy and haste. Through snow and ice he made his way to See-

konk, not far from the place where Blackstone lived.
Here Williams began to plant and build, and others
came to join him.

Fearing that trouble might arise with his Massachusetts neighbors, Governor Winslow advised Williams in
a friendly letter to go outside the Plymouth limits. Accordingly, Williams, with five others, went in a canoe
to look for another location. Tradition says that when

BLACKSTONE'S HOME.

these wanderers approached the eastern shore of Seekonk River they saw Indians who called out in English,
"What cheer, friends? What cheer?"

Going round a peninsula, Williams and his companions landed at the foot of a hill which he pitched
upon for his settlement. In gratitude for "God's merci-
ful providence to him in distress," he called this place
Providence.[2]

Between these several removals, Williams says that he was sorely tossed up and down, "not knowing for fourteen weeks what bed or bread did mean." But he was not friendless. His wife and children soon joined him. People began to find their way to the exile's home. Winslow came to visit him, and noting his old friend's distress he slipped a piece of gold in Mrs. Williams' hand when he went away.

BLACKSTONE'S GRAVE.

The Indians showed the exile great kindness. His knowledge of their language now stood him in good stead, for he may be said to have cast himself upon their mercy.

This place, which Williams gratefully called Providence, was claimed by Massasoit, who owned himself subject to Plymouth Colony; but Williams was told that he should not be disturbed. He bought the land of the natives over whom he soon gained great influence.

Williams afterward gave up his right to the whole body of settlers. They made a simple compact to abide by all such orders as the public good might require. These rules were to be established by a majority of the inhabitants duly assembled in Town-Meeting. Two deputies were to see to their enforcement. There was no hint of restraint of citizenship for conscience' sake.

[1] ROGER WILLIAMS was probably born in London, Eng. He was the friend of Cromwell, Vane and Milton. He wrote a few controversial tracts but nothing of equal value to his "Key" to the Indian tongue, which so aptly supplements Eliot's herculean labors in the same field. It is to be noted in estimating Williams that while detesting his opinions men like Winthrop and Winslow remained his friends. His generous forgetfulness of self when the several colonies were in danger is not his least claim to the title of public benefactor; nor is the fact of his exile less remarkable for having proved the salvation of the endangered plantations, for he alone was able to control the intractable Narragansetts. He is considered the founder of the Baptists in America.

[2] PROVIDENCE. Indian Mooshausick. Williams' landing-place at Slate Rock is held in affectionate veneration by Rhode Islanders. Sound judgment marked his selection of a site within reach of Boston and Plymouth and at the head of navigation rather than at some point lower down the bay. Until 1730 Providence included Smithfield, Gloucester and Scituate.

WARWICK PLANTATION.

A YEAR or more after Providence was settled, some of the people who had cattle moved a few miles further down the bay, keeping within Williams' purchase, to a place on the Pawtuxet, where good grazing was to be had in summer and hay for winter. They settled here.

Not long after, Samuel Gorton, an itinerant preacher who had been driven from Rhode Island, came among them. He proved a disturber of their peace. To rid themselves of Gorton the Pawtuxet people proffered their submission to Massachusetts. Gorton then bought Shawomet, or Warwick Neck, of Miantonimo and went there to live. He was still too near. Two petty sachems who thought themselves injured by the sale carried their complaint to Boston.[1] All the parties were ordered to appear there. Miantonimo went, but Gorton treated the summons with disdain.

Gorton had some followers of his own mind. His de-

fiance soon brought a company of soldiers to Shawomet
with order to take him at all hazards. He and his
friends shut themselves up in a house, barricaded it, and
declared that they would not be taken alive. The soldiers then fired on them, though without doing them any
hurt. After standing a short siege Gorton gave himself
up. He and his companions were first imprisoned, and

SHAWOMET.

then sent among several towns for safe keeping. This
was in October, 1643. When he was set free Gorton
went to England to seek redress, at which time he procured from the Earl of Warwick a patent to Shawomet
with which he hastened back to his old residence, thereafter called Warwick in honor of Gorton's noble patron.[2]

---

[1] READ WITH THIS the "Death of
Miantonimo."

[2] THIS CURIOUS CHAPTER shows us
that notwithstanding it promised the
fullest freedom of conscience Williams'
compact did not in practice always attain
that end.

RHODE ISLAND PLANTATIONS, 1637.

THE next to settle in Rhode Island were also exiles flying from religious persecution.

The Puritans had shown in Roger Williams' case how jealous they were of new or strange doctrines. It was only a year later that they were again troubled by the spread of novel opinions which the clergy styled heresies.

These so-called heresies originated in the church of Boston, and were advocated by some of the foremost men and women in the colony. At first, a great part of the church went with the new movement.

There was a very gifted but ambitious woman, named Anne Hutchinson,[1] who said the ministers did not preach sound doctrines to the people. It was then thought unseemly for women to mix in public affairs. Mrs. Hutchinson gave great offence by holding meetings in her house where women could talk over religious questions in private. She led all the rest in advocating the new doctrines and very many sided with her. And the town was presently drawn to one or the other side.

The dispute grew to a serious quarrel—so serious that the whole colony was divided into factions, for, or against, the new creed.[2] "Fierce speeches were spoken and some laid hands on others." The civil authorities then interfered. They first banished Rev. John Wheelwright. Then Mrs. Hutchinson was also exiled. Many prominent men were disfranchised and many more disarmed for upholding her. These severe measures were taken because it was feared that Mrs. Hutchinson's followers might make a revolution.

Driven to seek a home elsewhere, a company of eighteen travelled to Providence, where Roger Williams was. By his advice they went to the beautiful island called by the Indians Aquidneck, and by the whites Rhode Island,[3] which Williams helped them to buy of Canonicus. This was in March, 1637, old style.

Settling first at the northern end of the island, so many came to join them that another settlement[4] was

OLD STONE MILL, NEWPORT, R.I.

begun by William Coddington[5] at the southern end, where there was a fine harbor, the next spring. The first settlement was called Portsmouth and the second Newport.

At first the islanders lived independently of their brethren at Providence, under a simple government of their own making, they too being without patent or charter. But in 1643 the three towns[6] obtained   a patent uniting them in one body under the name of Providence Plantations. For a long time neither the colonists of Plymouth nor Massachusetts would recognize these new plantations in any way. They continued however to flourish by reason of the coming of those who thought the Puritan rule too strict.

[1] ANNE HUTCHINSON was the daughter of Rev. Francis Marbury. She married William Hutchinson of Lincolnshire, Eng., who brought his family to New England in the autumn of 1634. When his wife was exiled he sold his property in Boston and went with her to Rhode Island, taking a prominent part in the settlement there. Soon after his death the widow removed to New Rochelle. The Indians massacred the whole family, except one daughter, who was carried into captivity.

[2] THE NEW CREED, or Familism, as it was sometimes called, held that no one could be a Christian unless he had received an inward revelation of the Spirit.

[3] RHODE ISLAND. From Rhodes in the Levant. The name is usually referred to the year 1644, but Roger Williams says that Aquidneck was so-called "by us" in 1636.

[4] ANOTHER SETTLEMENT. Palfrey thinks that trouble among the settlers at Portsmouth led to this early division.

[5] WILLIAM CODDINGTON, a wealthy merchant, was the leading man in this emigration. His high position in Massachusetts Colony with the prominent part he took in these troubles caused his selection as first governor of Rhode Island Plantations.

[6] THREE TOWNS. Besides these, about 1641 Richard Smith set up the first trading-house in the Narraganset country in what is now Wickford, and some few people settled in the neighborhood, on particular grants obtained from the Indians.

THE PEQUOT WAR, 1637.

SOMETHING has been said already about the Pequots and their behavior towards the English and Dutch. Notwithstanding their losses by disease the Indians still outnumbered the English four to one. Therefore the English were always afraid that the Indians might combine to attack them.

The Pequot country proper was not very extensive. It was originally only a narrow strip between the Pawcatuck and Thames; but, as we have said, these

Pequots had overrun the country as far west as the Connecticut, and but for the whites they would have remained masters of it. The nation mustered about one thousand fighting men, who had two strong forts[1] to retreat to whenever their country should be invaded.

Now war with them would put these infant Connecticut settlements in great danger, because the Pequots could assail them with their whole power before any

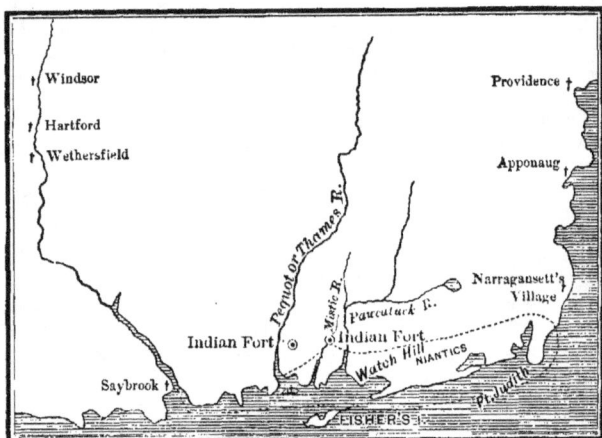

PLAN OF THE PEQUOT CAMPAIGN, 1637.

[The dotted lines show the route taken by our forces who, after their victory, marched to Pequot Harbor (New London), where their vessels met them.]

help could come. And this help was no nearer than Plymouth or Boston. So the situation of Connecticut Colony was truly one of great danger in case of war, since in the four towns[2] there were not more than three hundred fighting men, if indeed there were so many.

These settlers knew that if war broke out the Pequots would fall upon them the first and perhaps destroy them. It is true that the Pequots had the Narragan-

setts at their backs who were their most inveterate
enemies; but would the Narragansetts fight with the
English against their own countrymen? Would they
not rather lay aside their old enmity and join with the
Pequots?

So we see that the Tarratines were enemies of the
Massachusetts, the Massachusetts of the Narragansetts,
the Narragansetts of the Pequots, while the Iroquois
were enemies of all the rest. It was clearly to the interest of the English to keep alive these divisions and
so prevent the Indians acting together.

War broke out with the Pequots while Massachusetts
was banishing her people for heresy. It began in this
way:

Some roving Narragansetts had killed a trader named
Oldham[3] at Block Island. Oldham belonged to Watertown, so Massachusetts had to call his murderers to
account for the deed. Some of them were killed, and
some fled to the Pequots because their own friends, the
Narragansetts, washed their hands of the act.

Then Governor Vane and his council resolved to
chastise the Block Island Indians for this murder, and
the Pequots also, unless they would give good satisfac-
tion for their part in it. It was thought that a show
of force would intimidate them.

Accordingly drums were beaten for volunteers. A
hundred men were quickly mustered. With these Captain Endicott sailed for Block Island [4] in August, 1636.
His orders were to put to death all the men, but to
spare the women and children.

While the English were wading through the surf to
the shore, the Indians made a spirited attempt to drive
them back to their boats. Their arrows riddled the

clothing and rattled against the invaders' helmets like
hail-stones. Many a stout soldier owed his life that day
to wearing armor, for his arms were of no use in the
surf. As the English closed with them, however, the
Indians took to flight. Fourteen were killed. After
burning some cornfields and wigwams, the expedition
crossed over the Sound to Pequot River.[5] Here Endicott talked with some Pequots, but could get no satis-
faction from them. Seeing they were hostile he bade
them depart, for he was now come to fight them as they
had often dared the English to do. His men then had
a skirmish with them in which two Indians were killed.
Some wigwams also were burnt. Endicott then went
back to Boston, leaving his work not half done.

Because, instead of frightening them, this act served
only to enrage the Pequots. "You raise these wasps
around us and then flee away," said the poor terrified
Connecticut settlers to their Massachusetts brethren.
And they had good cause. Before a month went by
the Pequots were killing every settler who stirred outside his dooryard. Those who were taken were put to
cruel torture. Some were roasted alive, some hung up
on trees, where their friends could see them, yet so
mangled as hardly to be recognized when found.

Growing bolder, the Pequots lurked in ambush around
Saybrook fort and one day surprised a party while at
work outside. Four were killed before they could get
back into it. In order to show what an arrow shot
with skill could do, the captain of the fort sent Governor Vane a man's rib-bone with the arrow that had
killed him still sticking in it so firmly that it could not
be pulled out.

A few days later, three hundred Pequots openly beset

the fort. They dared the English to come out and
fight them; also mocking them by imitating the cries
of those poor prisoners whom they had tortured. A

well-aimed volley of grapeshot scattered them in terror.
Then the marauders drew off from the fort, but continued their bloody work of cutting off the settlers one by

one, shooting cattle, destroying crops, burning houses and the like until the poor settlers were as good as besieged in their several villages.

During the winter the Pequots tried to bring their old enemies, the Narragansetts, into a league with them against the English. "Join us or the English will first destroy us and then you," was the way they reasoned. And it was a prophecy.

Roger Williams heard what the Pequots were doing. Knowing that should they prevail the whites would have two thousand enemies upon them instead of one, he hastened alone to the Narragansett chiefs. He found them wavering and sullen. Canonicus reproached the English with having sent the plague among his people. Williams showed great courage. He freely mixed with the Pequot messengers whose evil looks showed how much his coming had angered them. In the end the old enmity proved strongest. Williams triumphed. So the Pequot emissaries went away full of hatred.

Besides the Pequots, there were the Mohegans and Niantics.[6]   The Mohegans dwelt on the west bank of the Thames, and though tributaries of the Pequots, they were on bad terms with them. So the Mohegans now joined the English against their old masters. The Niantics held aloof, though friendly to the Pequots.

Much English blood had been spilled. All the colonies agreed to make a determined effort to crush the Pequots before they should do more harm. Connecticut raised ninety men, all of whom were eager to meet the enemy. Captain John Mason,[7] a tried soldier, led them. At Saybrook, Captain Underhill joined him with twenty more. Besides the English, Uncas, the Mohegan chief, brought seventy of his braves to fight on their side.

With this little army Mason took the field in May against Sassacus and all his power.

He sailed first for Narragansett Bay. His object was to destroy the Pequot stronghold at Mystic by attacking it from the rear, and his plan was to deceive the Pequots. But to do this he must march through the Narragansett country. When his little band had landed, the Narragansetts spoke with scorn of the foolhardiness of going against Sassacus with so few men. " You dare not look a Pequot in the face," they said to the handful of whites. They however furnished four hundred warriors, though, at best, they were only half-hearted allies.

Meaning to surprise the Pequots

NINIGRET, A NIANTIC SACHEM.

Mason marched without delay, for every moment was precious. Coming undiscovered to within striking distance of the fort the English were halted for battle. Sounds of high revel could be heard in the English camp, as the Pequot scouts had seen Mason's vessels go past and no one thought of danger near. So the savages were lulled into fatal security.

The fort stood on the brow of a hill. It was a row of

stockades, twelve feet high, set in a ring, with entrances opposite each other. In it were seventy wigwams. Both entrances were blocked up with brushwood,

PORTER'S ROCKS, MYSTIC, CONN., WHERE MASON BIVOUACKED.

through which the assailants must force their way before they could get inside.

It was midnight before the Pequots had grown quiet.

The English then got ready for the assault. At one in the morning, by the light of a splendid May moon, Captain Mason marched toward one entrance, while Captain Underhill led his men toward the other. They were to meet inside the fort and give no quarter to the foe. Through fear or treachery all the Indian allies, except Uncas, now skulked in the rear. Mason told them they might keep out of harm's way if they liked, but that his men had come to look the Pequots in the face.

All was silent as the English approached the fort. Not until they were within a few rods was any alarm given. Then a dog suddenly barked, and immediately after a Pequot sentinel shouted "Owanux! Owanux!" Giving the foe no time to rally, the English fired one volley and then charged sword in hand. Underhill's men hung back until one brave young soldier cried out, "If we may not enter, wherefore are we here?" He then led the way into the thickest of the fight.

The space inside was so crowded with wigwams that the combatants fought hand to hand. The number of enemies was constantly increasing. The English hewed a way on with their swords, for firearms could not be used in the darkness, yet the press of enemies was so great, and their resistance so determined, that the two detachments never met. Finding that he would be beaten out of the fort, Mason seized a firebrand and thrust it among the dry mats of the nearest wigwam. Others did the same. The fire so quickly spread from hut to hut that the whole fort was soon in flames. This decided the day. The rest was mere butchery. English and Indians surrounded the blazing fortress, and by its light shot down, or drove back into the flames, all who tried to escape. In one hour the dreaded Pequot fort was in ashes. Between six and seven hundred had perished by fire and sword. Only seven were taken alive. Only two English were killed, but twenty had been wounded.

Though this victory did not actually end the war, it completely broke the Pequots' power. There were, it is true, further combats, but after this great disaster the Pequots broke up into small bands, who were hunted

STORMING THE PEQUOT FORT.

down without mercy. Sassacus fled to the Mohawks who basely slew him. Mononotto, the last great sachem, with a few followers retreated to a point of land now in Guilford. He was taken, beheaded, and his head set upon a tree, from which event the place has always been called Sachem's Head.

The destruction of Mystic Fort was a most daring feat of arms which deservedly raised the fame of the

English very high among the Indians, who had believed the Pequots invincible. It opened the Pequot country to settlement and was the means of securing a long period of peace.

[1] TWO STRONG FORTS. The principal one, and royal residence of Sassacus, was situated on Fort Hill in Groton, four miles east of New London. The other was on Pequot Hill, on the west side of the Mystic, near Mystic Village.

[2] THE FOUR TOWNS were Saybrook, Wethersfield, Hartford and Windsor.

[3] JOHN OLDHAM, who had also lived at Plymouth and Nantasket. He is almost ubiquitous.

[4] BLOCK ISLAND (Indian Manisses) was in 1672 made a township with the name of New Shoreham.

[5] PEQUOT RIVER. Thames River.

[6] NIANTICS. The chief seat of Ninigret, sachem of the Niantics, was in Westerly. The tribe formed an intermediate link between Pequots and Narragansetts with whom it was closely allied by blood.

[7] JOHN MASON had served in the Low Countries. He had removed from Dorchester to Windsor when the emigration to Connecticut began. After the Pequot War he wrote an account of it.

VI.

THE ERA OF PROGRESS.

FOUNDING OF HARVARD COLLEGE, 1636.

IT is to the lasting credit of Massachusetts that while engaged in war she should have fostered education. It shows that the men of that day had high and noble aims. One of them very clearly explains the motives which led to the founding of a college at so early a time. He says that, after they had crossed the sea, had built houses and churches, provided for getting a living, and settled their civil government, the next thing thought of was the advancement of learning.

Chiefly they wished to educate young men for the ministry, so as when those ministers[1] who had come from England died, others would be ready to take their places.

So in October, 1636, the colony set apart four hundred pounds toward building a college. The next year Newtown was chosen as the place for building it; and the next (1638), that town gave land for the site. Then the name of Newtown was changed to Cambridge, in honor of the university town of the same name in England.

At that time there lived in Charlestown a young Puritan minister named John Harvard. He was the son of Robert Harvard,[2] butcher, of the parish of St. Saviour's, Southwark, London. This young Harvard was a graduate of Cambridge University, England. He came to New England, and shortly after he fell ill and died. It was then found that he had left half his estate and all his books to the proposed college. It is true that the legacy would not be thought large in these days of great wealth, but it was then a very large sum. For this generous gift the Court gave the college its benefactor's name, Harvard College.

The first building was of wood. In it was a hall for commons, lectures and exercises; also a library, and chambers, and studies for the students' use. It was thought by some to be "too gorgeous for a wilderness," while others said it was too mean for a college. At best it was but an humble edifice, although the builders seemed very proud of it.

By the side of the college building stood a "faire grammar schoole" for the training up of the town youth and the fitting them for college.

We know that much interest was felt in the success of the college because many great and small gifts followed Harvard's generous one. Perhaps an appeal was made to the public for aid in the good work, as some gave money, some books, and others silver or pewtesr articles; while others, who could spare none of these things, sent live sheep for the commons' table, or home-spun cloth for the students' garments, every thing being honestly set down against the giver's name in the college book.

The first master, Nathaniel Eaton, was dismissed for

cruelty to the students. He then ran away. Henry
Dunster (1640) was the first who took the title of President. The first class of nine was graduated in 1642.
One of the graduates was William Hubbard,[3] the eminent historian and divine.

[1] MINISTERS. Collectively the Puritan ministers formed the ablest body that
has ever emigrated to any country. They
were mostly men of liberal education,
high character and superior intelligence.
The influence of such men in creating
society must not be overlooked, for whatever else it might lack every little community had its patriarch who was looked
up to with the greatest veneration.

[2] JOHN HARVARD. Very recently the
mystery surrounding his parentage has
been cleared up.

[3] WILLIAM HUBBARD wrote a narrative of the Indian wars (Boston 1677):
also a "History of New England," (Cambridge, 1815), printed after his death.
The first-named publication was also
reprinted in London the same year,
1677.

FIRST PRINTING-PRESS IN NEW ENGLAND, 1639.

HARVARD COLLEGE had the first printing-press in
North America. Upon the college records we read this
item: "Mr. Joss Glover gave to the college a font of
printing-letters, and some gentlemen of Amsterdam gave
towards furnishing a printing-press."

Printing had been done for the priests in Mexico a
century before, but this Cambridge Press was the first
one set up in the English colonies.

The Rev. Josse Glover was a dissenting, or Puritan,
minister, in England, who seems to have set his mind
upon being the founder of printing in New England,
for he came himself with the types and press.[1] Having
engaged a printer named Stephen Daye he sailed with
his family in 1638 for Boston. Most unfortunately, Mr.
Glover died on the voyage, but the rest of the company,

with the press, arrived at Cambridge in the autumn. And there the "printery," as some called it, was set up, in President Dunster's house. By and by Mr. Dunster married the widow Glover, "so taking her, as well as the press, into his own house."

Daye's want of skill cost him his place of printer to which his son Matthew succeeded: and after him (1649) Samuel Green, a better printer than either, took charge.

The "Freeman's Oath," printed by S. Daye, in 1639, on one side of a small sheet of paper, was the first thing printed with types in what are the United States. The second and third issues were almanacs, for the years 1639 and 1640. The next was a much more important work.

This was the first book printed. It was entitled "The Whole Booke of Psalmes Faithfully translated into English metre," and is dated 1640. For brevity's sake it is usually called

EARLY PRINTING-PRESS.

the Bay Psalm Book and is so very uncommon that a copy is worth many times its weight in gold.

Before this time the Pilgrim and Puritan churches used Sternhold and Hopkins' version of the Psalms, but the want of a better one seems to have been so strongly felt that two ministers, Thomas Welde and John Eliot, were appointed to make it. One specimen of their poetic style will give an idea of the church singing of that time when each line was separately read by a deacon before it was sung by the congregation.

"The Lord to mee a Shepheard is,
want therefore shall not I.
Hee in the folds of tender-grasse
doth cause mee downe to lie.
To waters calme me gently leads
Restore my soule doth hee:
he doth in paths of righteousnes
for his names sake lead me."

The celebrated translation of the Bible into the Indian tongue was also printed on the Cambridge Press, but that work belongs to a later day than the one now being considered.

So we see that the colonists were for some time without other means of duplicating public documents than that of copying them by hand. And this work was done by persons called Scriveners.[2] Instead of leaving a copy at every householder's door, one was usually nailed to the door of the meeting-house, the doing which gave it a lawful publication.

[1] PRINTING-PRESS. Efforts to trace this press have proved unavailing. After doing duty for nearly a century it was probably broken up.

[2] SCRIVENERS, writers, or scribes, were the "copyists" of that day, when ability to write a good hand was so rare an accomplishment that "writers" were generally men above the common rank of society.

ANCIENT AND HONORABLE ARTILLERY COMPANY, 1637.

THIS celebrated corps was formed during the Pequot War, on the plan of a similar one in London. Composed only of the best citizens, it was meant rather for home defence, and for training up young soldiers, than for active service. As the special bulwark of the State, great pains were taken to maintain a high standard of discipline. It is now the oldest military body in America.

NEW HAVEN COLONY, 1638.

A COMPANY of people of whom Theophilus Eaton[1] and John Davenport[2] were the leaders, arrived at Boston during the Pequot War. After some hesitation they concluded to go and settle at Quinipiack,[3] a harbor

OLD STONE HOUSE, GUILFORD, CONN.

of Long Island Sound, lying some ten or twelve leagues west of the Connecticut.

It took them a fortnight to make the voyage thither. Their first Sabbath was kept under an oak tree, Mr. Davenport preaching to them upon Christ's temptation in the wilderness. They then set about forming a civil compact in which they agreed to make the Bible their code of laws. The framers of this compact met in a barn. It was settled that none except church-members should be freemen of this colony. Seven men, who were called the Seven Pillars, were chosen to begin a church. They, with other church-members, then took up civil matters, and elected Eaton their chief magistrate. Afterwards they gave their town the name of New Haven.

In this way another little free State was formed, for New Haven was at first independent of all other Connecticut settlements. The colonists were mostly well to do. They did not suffer from want or savage warfare, as they had come in just as the Pequots had been driven out. So their colony was soon in a flourishing condition.

Very soon (1639) a large company, partly from New Haven and partly from Wethersfield, removed still farther west to the mouth of the Housatonic,[4] and settled Milford. Another party went in the opposite direction and founded Guilford.[5] Each place was under its own government, and formed a separate commonwealth.

Erelong all these scattered towns were brought within one or the other colony. The next year Fairfield and Stratford were settled, and came under Connecticut Colony. Saybrook also joined Connecticut. Southampton, Long Island,[6] and Stamford were settled, the first by new-comers (1640), the second by Wethersfield people (1641). These two places, with Milford and Guilford, annexed themselves to New Haven, and from that time they sent their deputies to the General Court there. Springfield being found to lie in Massachusetts, her people withdrew from Connecticut and joined Massachusetts.

---

[1] THEOPHILUS EATON was a London merchant.

[2] JOHN DAVENPORT, a Puritan minister, educated at Oxford, Eng. Persecution drove him first to Holland and subsequently to America. Was one of the "Seven Pillars" chosen by the New Haven colonists.

³ QUINIPIACK, Indian name of New Haven.
⁴ HOUSATONIC (Indian) signifying "over the mountain."
⁵ GUILFORD (Indian Menuncatue), settled by Rev. Henry Whitefield and forty others. William Leet was the first civil magistrate.
⁶ LONG ISLAND. The natives were said to be very treacherous and warlike. Their war canoes would carry eighty men across the Sound and their wampum was considered the best in the country. The original settlers of Suffolk County were mostly from New England. In 1644 Southampton was also annexed to the jurisdiction of Connecticut. Trouble arose with the Dutch who occupied what is now King's County. Later, the island was transferred to New York.

MARTHA'S VINEYARD AND NANTUCKET, 1642,¹

WE have told how Martha's Vineyard came to be discovered and named. Far back in the early days this island went by the Indian name of Capawock.

Epenow, an Indian belonging to this island, had been kidnapped and carried off to England. Being a man of great stature, he was shown up and down London as a wonder. To get his liberty Epenow told marvellous stories about mines of gold to be found in his island home, to all of which his captors eagerly listened. Even Sir Ferdinando Gorges was so much deceived that he sent a ship to secure the gold, and Epenow went in her to show where it was.

But Epenow was a crafty fellow. When the ship came to the island, she was speedily boarded by natives with whom Epenow freely talked. In order to prevent his escaping from them the English had put long garments on him, and two of them always stood ready to lay hands on him should he offer to get away. Epenow had laid his plans cunningly. His clansmen surrounded the ship in their canoes, and when the chance came, he broke away from his guards and leaped into the sea. Then all the Indians let fly their arrows at once. The ship's company fired upon them with their muskets, but the Indians fought so resolutely that Epenow made good his escape.

Some time after, the Indians attacked another of Gorges' captains who landed on the island with only a few men. Epenow led this attack. All the whites were slain except the captain, who got back to his boat sorely wounded.

For many years no whites thought of settling upon the island. The Indians were looked upon as being the most savage, cruel and treacherous of their race. Hardly could the whites yet call themselves masters on the main, nor did any one seriously think of Martha's Vineyard as a place of abode until the Pequot War had cowed the Indians everywhere.

Then, in 1641, Thomas Mayhew of Watertown, Mass., was granted the islands of Martha's Vineyard and Nantucket. With his son Thomas, and a few others, he went to the Vineyard (1642), which was then full of Indians. The younger Mayhew[2] at once set about converting them to Christianity. What seemed a hopeless task soon bore fruit. In time the natives were turned from their savage ways, and many converted. Mayhew's first convert was an Indian named Hiacoomes, who afterward became an eminent preacher to his own people.

NANTUCKET[3] was not settled until long after. It also was a very populous island whose inhabitants were very dexterous and daring watermen. But wanting a good soil it did not invite settlers like the fertile meadows of the Connecticut or the Housatonic. It also lacked harbors; nor could mariners approach its engulfing shoals without danger of shipwreck. Therefore, so late as 1643, the natives held sole sway over the whole island.

The Indians had many legends touching these islands. One was that Nantucket was formed of the ashes which the Indian god Maushope emptied from his pipe, and that the fogs were caused by his smoking.

[1] BOTH ISLANDS belonged to Maine (Sir F. Gorges' grant, 1639) with a presumptive title in Sir William Alexander (Earl of Stirling) through Gorges. Both sold to Mayhew. By order of the United Colonies (1644) Martha's Vineyard was annexed to Massachusetts.

[2] THE YOUNGER MAYHEW was lost at sea. Williams, Eliot and Mayhew are a noble triumvirate in our annals. Their humane methods were found more potent than the sword in solving the Indian question of their day.

[3] NANTUCKET is a word probably of Indian origin. It was settled by Quakers from Salisbury, Mass.

DISCOVERY OF THE WHITE MOUNTAINS, 1642.

Up to this time exploration of the interior had made little progress. Neal, as we have seen, had not succeeded in finding the great beaver lake. Yet it is reported that in 1636 a Captain Young, with only three companions, went up the Kennebec, to make discovery of that river, under the supposition that it ran out of this

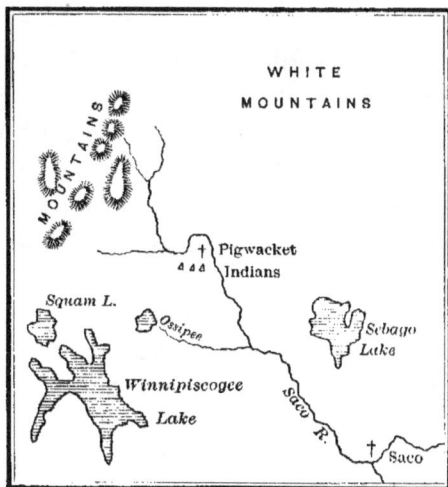

ROUTE OF EARLY EXPLORERS.

wonderful great lake. By carrying their canoes over

short portages, Young's party finally reached the great river St. Lawrence. Young was taken by the French who sent him to France, but his companions came safely home again.

The whites knew that far away in the north there was a cluster of very high mountains, for they had often seen them, but the mountains were so distant that no white man had ever visited them. Moreover, much mystery attached to them. The Indians said that their god dwelt high up among those lofty peaks, and told marvellous stories about great shining stones that glittered on the cliffs through the darkness of night. Now and then they would show a piece of crystal which they said came from the greatest mountain. So the whites at first called it the Crystal Hill.

"But," said the Indians to the whites, "nobody can go to the top of Agiochook, to get these glittering stones, because it is the abode of the great god of storms, famine and pestilence. Once, indeed, some foolish Indians had attempted to do so, but they had never come back, for the spirit that guarded the gems from mortal hands had raised great mists, through which the hunters wandered on like blind men until the spirit led them to the edge of some dreadful gulf, into which he cast them shrieking."

There was one bold settler who was determined to go in search of the precious stones, cost what it might. His name was Darby Field.

So in June, 1642, Field started to go to the Crystal Hill. When he came to the neighborhood of the present town of Fryeburg, he found an Indian village there. It was the village of the Pigwackets, or as it is sometimes written, Pequawketts.[1]

Here Field took some Indian guides who led him to within a few miles of the summit when, for fear of the

AMONG THE MOUNTAINS.

evil spirit, all but two refused to go farther. So Field went on with these two.

They clambered resolutely over rocks and among scrubby savins, no higher than a man's knee, to a sort of stony plain where there were two ponds. Above this plain, rose the great peak of shattered rocks that over-looks all New England. This too they climbed.

Field has said that the sight of the great wilderness land stretched out all around him, the mountains falling away beneath his feet into dark gulfs, was "daunting terrible." It is so to-day.

Field stood upon the great watershed of New England. Finding the day far spent he began searching for the precious stones he had come so far to seek. He found a few crystals which he brought away, thinking them to be diamonds. He also found a deal of "Muscovy glass," or isinglass, adhering to the rocks. Some of this he also took with him. With his treasures Field then came down the mountain to the place where he had left the Indians, whom he found drying themselves by a fire, for while he was above the clouds, a sudden storm had swept over them. As they had given up the adventurous pale face for lost, their wonder at seeing him return safe and sound was very great. All then went back to the Indian village.

[1] PEQUAWKETTS were driven from their ancient seat, after Lovewell's bloody fight, in 1725.

DEATH OF MIANTONIMO, 1643.

TOWARD the end of the year 1642 the English again grew uneasy concerning the attitude of the Indians. No hostile act on their part is mentioned, but it was said, and believed, that they were quietly arming for war. And as the Narragansetts were now much the most powerful Indian nation in New England, they were naturally regarded with most fear and distrust.

Uncas, the Mohegan sachem, who had fought on the side of the English against the Pequots, artfully sought to deepen this distrust of Miantonimo, the Narragansett chief, whom he both hated and feared, and as Miantonimo was thought most capable of planning and executing such a project, Uncas was nearly successful in making the English go to war with him. Some men had actually marched when cooler counsels prevailed, and they were recalled. Because a general rising of the Indians was expected to come sooner or later, there was always a party who favored exterminating them. This party was for immediate war.

DEATH OF MIANTONIMO.

But the Narragansetts had also proved themselves faithful allies in the war with the Pequots. To attack them then unawares, and unheard, would be most unjust. Yet it was important to know the truth. Orders were therefore sent out to the frontier towns to disarm all the Indians in their neighborhood, and send the head chiefs to Boston, that they might answer to this charge of conspiracy.

Among others Miantonimo came. He came fearlessly. His bearing was that of a chief who had made the English his allies, but would never allow them his peers. Now the respect felt for this ignorant savage's abilities was such that the governor and his councillors had found it needful to settle their plan of dealing with him beforehand. They decided among themselves what questions to ask him, and in what order they should be put, while Miantonimo was of course unprepared. Nothing came of it. The chief gave wary answers, weighed every word, and never spoke without first taking time for reflection. He demanded proof or else that his accusers should be punished for speaking falsely, according to Indian justice.

But no proof was produced—none, indeed, had been found. So Miantonimo easily cleared himself, though his manner showed how deeply he felt the indignity that had been put upon him at the instigation of Uncas, whom he promptly accused of being at the bottom of the matter.

When he was ready to go home, Miantonimo shook hands with the governor and such of the magistrates as were present, after the English form of leave-taking. Then going a little way off he came back to them, and gave his hand to the governor again, saying that it was for those magistrates who were absent. And so, for the present, war was happily averted.

The English, however, continued true to their policy of promoting divisions among the Indians themselves. Opportunities were not wanting. In a little while two petty Narragansett sachems, whom Miantonimo had offended, appealed to the English for protection. The English heard the cause and sustained the sachems in their defiance of Miantonimo. This act still further embittered him toward the English, though he wisely refrained from seeking revenge.

The next year Uncas made war on Sequasson, a Connecticut sachem, who was the kinsman and ally of Miantonimo. Uncas killed many of Sequasson's men, burnt their wigwams and carried off much booty. Hearing this, which was the same as a defiance, Miantonimo hastened to the aid of Sequasson, though not

MIANTONIMO MONUMENT

before he had given notice of his march to the English. They seeing no cause to interfere, left the chiefs to fight it out between themselves.

Miantonimo invaded the Mohegan country at the head

of his warriors. He had the most men but Uncas' were the better armed. For the coming battle he put on a suit of English armor. In the first combat Miantonimo suffered defeat, and being weighed down by the armor he wore, was easily overtaken. His pursuers contented themselves with keeping him at bay until Uncas could come up, and have the honor of taking the great Narragansett. When Uncas laid his hand on Miantonimo's shoulder, the latter sat down in token of submission. He disdained to ask for mercy, but with Indian stoicism awaited his fate in silence. "Why do you not speak?"

WAR-CLUB AND AXE.

asked Uncas. "If you had taken me, I would have besought you to spare my life."

When it was known that Miantonimo was a prisoner, Gorton and other Englishmen whom he had befriended at once demanded his release. Uncas therefore took his prisoner to Hartford, and submitted the decision of the matter to the English Confederates. In secret council they determined that Miantonimo should be put to death, but in such manner that the responsibility should rest with Uncas alone.

Uncas readily undertook the execution of this cruel sentence. Accordingly, the captive was delivered up to him, and while marching along with his guards was instantly killed by the blow of a tomahawk. So died the noblest Indian that had yet appeared in New England.[1]

¹ SACHEM'S PLAIN, near Norwich, is the scene alike of the battle between the rival chiefs and of Miantonimo's execution. For many years every Indian who passed the spot added a stone to the heap over his grave, as their custom was. In time this rude monument was succeeded by a block of granite, simply inscribed. It is certain that without Miantonimo's protection no Englishman could have settled in Rhode Island and it is doubtful whether the Pequots could have been overcome without his aid. The opportunity of ridding themselves of so formidable a leader was eagerly seized upon by the English and must stand as the one pretext for his assassination.

THE COLONISTS AT WORK.

FIRST of all every colonist needed a house to shelter him. Therefore artisans of all sorts were most in demand. Carpenters, joiners, masons or tilers, brickmakers, blacksmiths and sawyers, found instant employment at their several trades; and to avoid oppression of the poor man, the wages of labor were at first regulated by law.

As husbandry was the natural resource of all, every man was a farmer. In order to live he had to be a producer. Each colonist had been told to bring with him sufficient provision of bread or meat to last until his first crop should be gathered in, but not many were provident enough to do so and others lacked means. So only those who brought cows, goats and fowls had the means of living ready at hand.

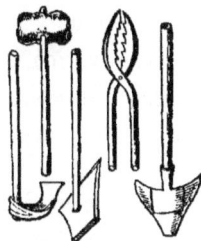

AGRICULTURAL IMPLEMENTS, 1620.

Their milk, butter, cheese and eggs were luxuries which most people had to do without.

In the larger towns, like Boston and Salem, all milch-cows and goats were put in charge of a public cowherd who drove them forth at morning to the common pasture and at night back to their owners. Horses and oxen, of which there were at first but few, were put to work hauling timber, stones. earth or other materials from place to place.

CHEESE-PRESS.

Each citizen had a plot of ground set apart to him for his houselot and garden. At Boston the example of the Pilgrims in laying out fields in which all should share the work of planting, and all have a portion of the crop, was first followed. This plan best economized labor, and excellently answered the temporary purpose of getting bread quickly, but it limited production too much, for the reasons given in the Pilgrims' case. Commonage was put in practice everywhere.[1]

There were wealthy colonists who became entitled to larger grants in return for money advanced, which grants accordingly were made to them next the towns, in situations where a due proportion of planting, pasturage and woodland could be had. The poorer sort of people were allowed to plant on these large farms on the condition that the owners should have all the improvements these

WOOL-WHEEL.

tenants might make on their lands. The tenant worked until he was able to buy a homestead for himself. The owner saw his unproductive land made valuable by the tenant's labor. The country had the benefit of a larger breadth of planted land.

Every man's hand found work to do in felling trees, burning brushwood, picking up stones, grubbing up roots, fencing or ploughing his planting-ground. Idleness was more than a fault, it was a crime punished by setting the offender at work at the hardest labor to be found.

The Pilgrims had first proved the capabilities of the soil for growing English rye, barley, pease and beans. Corn was the native Indians' great bread crop. But inasmuch as there was not a work animal of any kind in Plymouth Colony for years, so all the labor of tilling the ground had to be performed by hand, with hoe and spade. Not much could be done in this way. The later comers, however, brought over ploughs[2] of the kind then in use in England, which was a very clumsy affair with wheels to draw it by.

But the pride of every family was its kitchen garden. Perhaps no one thing gave so much true delight as tending the little patch of ground in which the first trial of the carefully hoarded seeds was being made. In a very few years the colonists had vegetables in great abundance. One of the earliest travellers in New England has told us that he saw turnips, carrots, radishes, onions, squashes, cucumbers, pumpkins and melons growing everywhere by the side of the settlers' cottages.

Besides what was strictly for food uses, a prudent foresight taught these people that they would soon want articles of clothing. England was far and everything dear. And nothing was so scarce as money. Flax and

hemp were therefore early sown for domestic use. In
Connecticut the planting of these two things was made
obligatory on every family.
Hops were also generally
cultivated for making beer,
which was drank by all
classes of people.

LOOM.

A few wise men planted
orchards, some relics of
them being still seen in
the older settlements.
There is a tradition that
Blackstone had one at Boston; but it is known that
after him, Winthrop and Endicott took the lead in setting out fruit trees, as they also had done in every work
of practical utility or benevolence.

We have just now spoken of those plants yielding
fibre for making cloth. Among laboring people leather
to some extent took the place of cloth. His leather
jerkin, breeches and leggins was the laborer's every-day
garb. Still, looking ahead to the future, an absolute
need of providing for coming
wants led to the offering of a
bounty on every yard of cotton,[3]
woollen or linen cloth that
should be produced in the colony of Massachusetts. Every-
body who could afford the ex-
pense got a spinning-wheel.
To wear a dress wholly home-
spun, as well as home-made,

SPINNING-WHEEL.

was thought a meritorious thing. This was the first
protected industry in New England. It was an

early step toward making her independent and prosperous.

Leather being an article of prime necessity, Francis
Ingalls started the first tannery in the colony, at Lynn,
with what hides could be picked up in the country.
Salem led in the manufacture of pottery, John Pride
having begun it there about 1641.

Other manufactures were chiefly directed to home
wants. The building of saw and grist mills was among
those works of pressing necessity which had immediate
attention. Those who lived in the out settlements had
to trudge many a weary mile to mill with what corn
they could carry on their backs, or in winter draw on a
hand-sled of home manufacture. It is true, some families owned an iron or wooden mortar in which the grain
was pounded in the Indians' way: but the labor was
too great and the process too slow for general use.

The colonists also turned their attention to the various uses to which the timber growing at their doors
could be put, for they rightly accounted it one of their
greatest sources of wealth.

Sawed boards were everywhere in demand. So were
shingles, clapboards and palings, which the farm hands
made in the winter months with a hand-saw, a froe, and
a hatchet.[4] By and by they made pipe-staves also, and
with these, their lumber, and their dry fish the colonists
began trading in a modest way with the West Indies,
receiving sugar, spices, raisins, tropical fruits and many
other luxuries, in exchange for their own commodities.

Ship-building,[5] or rather boat-building, was another
work of primary importance, and its rise marks the ad-
vancing steps the colony was taking, not only in thrift,
but toward opening an intercourse with the outside

world. Shallops, ketches, pinnaces, lighters and small boats were first built. These were for the coast trade and fishery. Then followed ships of one, two and even three hundred tons burden,—all being laden with New England commodities destined for Spain, Portugal, or the West Indies. The going forth of a ship on such a voyage was then an event of the greatest importance and solemnity. Prayers were offered up at her depart-

CHURN, WOOL-WHEEL AND HAND-REEL.

ure, as there was no likelihood of her being heard from until her return to the home port.

So out of some grove of tall pines or sturdy oaks was wrought a brave ship, freighted with home products and manned by home-made sailors. New England was afloat upon the seas, bearing messages of her own industry to all the nations of the earth.

Finding plenty of bog-iron ores everywhere in the meadows and shallow ponds, John Winthrop Jr. went over to England in order to get help to build a forge. He was successful, returning in 1643 with money and workmen. Works were begun the same year at Lynn, on the banks of the Saugus River.

But neither of these was the one great industry of New England. That was the cod-fishery.

Though an armed Indian appears on the shield of Massachusetts, the admitted importance of the fishery, as the chief source of her wealth, led to the adoption of a codfish as her peculiar symbol, and accordingly one was hung up in the colonial Chamber of Representatives at an early day, and is still hanging in the State House at Boston, to remind her people what they owe to this humble denizen of the sea. So when New England sent her delegates to attend the great council-fire of the Iroquois, they took with them the wooden model of a codfish as their token, or credentials, which was handed round among the sachems, and kept by them to show that New England had thus pledged herself to keep the league with them; for the New Englanders knew that the Iroquois called their country Kinshon, that is a fish, from its greatest industry.

Turning to other and minor avocations that belong to the domestic life of a people, we find soap-boilers, tinkers, tailors, glovers, coopers, shoemakers, curriers, glaziers, millers, tallow-chandlers, and even barber-surgeons plying their several occupations in the infant colonies. With regard to the public weal inns were licensed. Watchmen went their nightly rounds crying the hour and weather. The tax-gatherer made his unwelcome visits. Train-bands were formed, in which boys of fourteen were mustered for military exercise with men. And no citizen was allowed to sue another until he should first have submitted his cause to some of the magistrates. What sagacity in the rulers, fru-

gality in people and commonwealth had done in thirteen
years, will be told in the next chapter.

---

¹ COMMONAGE was one of the oldest
of old customs. Though always a pro-
lific cause of contention it has survived
at Nantucket and Long Island, where
people lived simply, and largely by their
flocks. Boston Common furnishes an
example of land so held to-day.

² PLOUGHS. The Indians thought the
first ploughman they saw was a wizard.
A stone hoe or large clam-shell fixed to
a handle were their implements of husbandry.

³ COTTON. The first raw cotton was
brought to New England from Barba-
does. The people of Rowley, Mass.,
were the first cloth-workers.

⁴ TOOLS. A broad-axe for hewing, a
felling-axe and grindstone were indis-
pensable to every farmer.

⁵ SHIP-BUILDING. Governor Winthrop launched the "Blessing of the
Bay" in 1631. Governor Cradock's men
had a vessel of a hundred tons on the
stocks the next year at Medford. Salem,
Boston and Dorchester turned out many
large ships before 1642.

PROGRESS IN THE OLDER COLONIES.

THOUGH getting some increase from it, the Old
Colony had fallen far behind in the great emigration.
A few of those who were left at Leyden had indeed
come over and so had others. But the great tide had
rolled by her. Nor was this colony any longer one
town, one church and one citadel as in the beginning,
for so many had gone out from Plymouth to dwell upon
more fertile lands, some to the north and some to the
south.

They who first went out settled Duxbury; then
Marshfield, Scituate, Barnstable, Yarmouth, Sandwich
and Taunton were occupied. In 1643 there were in the
whole colony six hundred men able to bear arms, or not
far from three thousand people.

Their going was but the natural result of a more
robust growth. The younger men could no longer be
kept from seeking to better their condition, since the

country about them was being settled on all sides. But
the old Pilgrims looked with no favor upon this breaking up of their community, to the maintenance of which
they had consecrated their lives.

Beyond the Penobscot, Isaac Allerton,[1] of Plymouth,
had started an Indian trading-post where Machias now
is. The attempt was short-lived, for the French (1633)

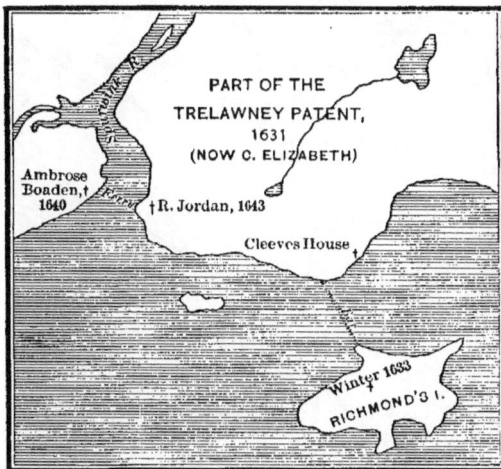

RICHMOND'S ISLAND AND CAPE ELIZABETH.

took both house and goods, killing two of Allerton's
men who made resistance.

Maine grew slowly. The French claim had shut out
settlement east of Pemaquid. That part remained a
sort of neutral ground. On the west, a solitary settler
had made his home (1639) where Brunswick now is.
Straggling hamlets were located at Richmond's Island,[2]
Portland, Scarborough, and in the neighborhood of
the Saco, and at Cape Porpoise. Wells had been settled

(1643) by Mr. Wheelwright whom we have seen exiled for his opinions. All of these plantations would not have made one good-sized town.

The New Hampshire plantations also made slow advance. Petty quarrels grew up among them which led to their seeking (1641) a union with Massachusetts

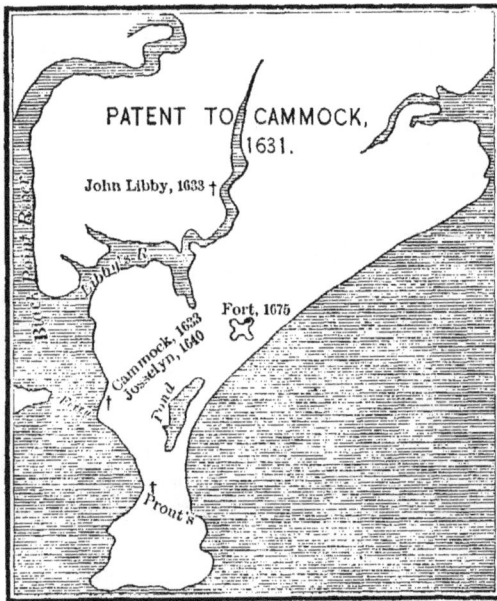

BLACK POINT OR SCARBOROUGH.

for the sake of peace and order. Exeter had been settled by Wheelwright and his friends, and Hampton (1638) by Massachusetts people, but as Massachusetts claimed both places Wheelwright quitted Exeter and went to Maine, as we have said.

Connecticut had withdrawn herself from the control of Massachusetts altogether. In the interior the people were all farmers, on the coast they were both farmers and fishermen.

Massachusetts had increased to thirty towns with her west frontier on the Connecticut, and her north reaching beyond the Merrimack.[3] In thirteen years each mother town had hatched out a numerous brood. These thirty towns were divided (1643) into four counties.[4]

But civil strife in England now put a stop to the voluntary exile of the Puritans. Indeed, they now called upon their brethren in New England to come over and help them fight the battle of religious freedom at home. And some of the ablest did go.

This new state of affairs put the several colonies wholly upon their own resources. There was no longer great demand for cattle, corn, lumber or such other products as were most wanted by new colonists. Accordingly, the prices of all such commodities fell one-half in value. Money grew scarce. Public and private expenditure halted. The people would not vote money except for works of prime necessity, nor themselves spend except for actual needs. The end of growth from outside help was the beginning of a new era of growth from the inside, and though progress was for a time checked, it soon moved forward on safer ground than before.

Massachusetts had also (1641) made a code of laws called "The Body of Liberties." Upon the demand of her freemen she had divided the General Court into two bodies, one being a popular branch, or House of Deputies, the other a board of magistrates or Councillors. Confusion had settled into order. Order brought prosperity. Prosperity wrought stability in the Commonwealth.

At this time, the wisest men conceived the idea of bringing all the New England colonies into a single confederacy.

[1] ISAAC ALLERTON, one of the Pilgrims, had been most prominent at Plymouth and much trusted until his mismanagement brought about a rupture with his old friends, who suspected him of working more zealously for his own advantage than theirs. He then became a sort of roving trader for which employment his knowledge of the coasts and country rendered him a formidable competitor of the Pilgrims. Point Allerton, at the entrance to Boston harbor, is named for him.

[2] RICHMOND'S ISLAND. Robert Trelawney, a merchant, had established his agent John Winter here in 1633, to carry on fishing and trading. Winter says it was no place for Indian trade because with exception of a few who lived about the Saco there were no Indians within fifty miles of him.

[3] MERRIMACK. Settlement had extended from Newbury to Salisbury, Haverhill (Indian Pentucket) and Andover (Indian Cochicawac).

[4] FOUR COUNTIES were Suffolk, Essex, Middlesex and Norfolk. The names originally signified geographical position, as Northfolk, Southfolk, etc. Norfolk has now different boundaries.

THE CONFEDERACY OF 1643.

WE have seen the gap between English and Dutch nearly closed. But they were never good neighbors. Since the English had as good as driven them from the Connecticut, the Dutch retaliated by expelling some English settlers from Long Island. There was growing hostility on both sides.

Then there were the French in Nova Scotia who kept up a defiant attitude. And there were also the Indians, with whom another and a harder struggle might come at any moment.

Lastly, war between king and Parliament made the colonists feel the need of drawing closer together, until stable government should be established again in England. A majority sided with the Parliament, but in Maine and Rhode Island perhaps more sympathy was felt for the royal cause.

All these motives led the colonies to seek a closer union with each other. After conference upon it Massachusetts, Plymouth, Connecticut and New Haven signed articles of union. The Maine and Rhode Island plantations were excluded because they and the others were not on good terms. Or perhaps it would be better to say that they differed so widely in government and religion that there could be little harmony between them.

The Confederates took the name of "The United Colonies of New England." It was a league for both war and peace, as mutual interest might demand. Each colony retained its own independence in all things though it was bound to help the others at need. And the relative number of men that each should furnish was agreed upon. If two hundred were wanted Massachusetts was to raise one hundred, while the quotas of the others were fixed at forty-five each.

The agreement, or confederation, was given effect by choosing two commissioners from each colony who formed a board for settling all questions that should come before it.

Thus, in 1643, the strength of the New England colonies stood united in a firm compact, not unlike that of the confederate Swiss Cantons. No government was established over the whole. Each member was left free to manage its own affairs, though ready to arm in its neighbor's defence. And with this league the making of New England was complete.

INDEX.

Acadie, French name for New England, 20; renewed attempts to settle, 51.

Agamenticus, Mt. (also Indian name of York), 127.

Agawam tribe, residence, 151; raided by Tarratines, 172; supported by English, 178.

Alden, John, tradition about, 83.

Algonquin traditions, 49, 50.

Allerton, Isaac, at Machias, 239, 242 (*note*).

Ancient and Honorable Artillery, when and how formed, 218.

Aquidneck. *See* Rhode Island, 202.

Argall, Samuel, at Mt. Desert, 54, 55 (*note*).

Arms and armor won by English, 37, 40 (*notes*); arquebuse, 46.

Arundel, Thomas, patron of a voyage to New England, 32.

Avocations of the people, 237.

Azores Islands, 9, 13 (*note*).

Baccalos, its meaning, 3.

Bandoleer described, 19 (*note*).

Barnstable settled, 238.

Basques, 11, 14 (*note*).

Bay Path, 193, 194 (*note*).

Beaver-skin, its commercial value, 19 (*note*).

Blackstone, Rev. William, first mentioned, 114; goes to Rhode Island, 181.

Block Island, discovered, 57, 58 (*note*); invaded, 205, 213 (*note*).

Block, Adrian, explores Long Island Sound, 56.

Boston, explored, 164; its landmarks, 166; Blackstone's location, 166; first settlers, 167; named, 167 and *note;* region first occupied, 168; first burial-place, 169; eminences named, 169; other sites, 168, 169; way of life, 170; struggle with want, 171; selected for public meetings, 174; first school, shop and inn, 181.

Bradford, William, first mentioned, 78; his wife drowned, 78; chosen governor, 96, 103 (*note*).

Brereton, John, with Gosnold, 12.

Brewster, William, first mentioned, 69.

Brunswick settled, 239.

Cambridge (Newtown), chosen for a colonial capital, 174; exodus from, to Connecticut, 192; chosen to found a college in, 214.

Canonicus sells the island of Rhode Island to whites, 202.

Cape Ann or Anna, mentioned, 62; Pilgrims at, 137; described, 138; Pilgrims abandon it, 139; abandoned by Conant, 141.

Cape Cod, visited and named, 12, 13; Mayflower puts into, 71; explored, 72; Indians of, 74–76; towns settled, 238.

Cape Elizabeth, 64 (*note*).

Carver, John, first mentioned, 69;

245

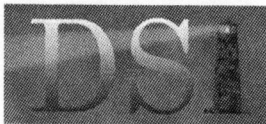

Other Colonial History titles offered by *Digital Scanning, Inc.*

New English Canaan,
by Jack Dempsey
As Published in 1999.
TP: 1582181519 ($29.95)
HC: 1582181500 ($39.95)

New English Canaan Text & Notes,
by Thomas Morton
Edited by Jack Dempsey
As Published in 1999.
TP: 158218206X ($15.95)
HC: 1582182078 ($27.95)

Thomas Morton of Merrymount,
by Jack Dempsey
As Published in 1999.
TP: 1582182094 ($21.95)
HC: 1582182108 ($34.95)

Good News From New England,
by Jack Dempsey
As Published in 2001.
TP: 1582187061 ($17.95)
HC: 158218707X ($31.95)

Massasoit of the Wampanoags,
by Alvin G. Weeks
As Published in 1920.
TP: 1582185921 ($14.95)
HC: 158218593X ($27.95)

The History of Philip's War,
by Thomas Church, Esq.
As Published in 1827.
TP: 158218089X ($19.95)
HC: 1582181306 ($29.95)

History of King Philip,
by John Abbott
As Published in 1857.
TP: 1582183147 ($19.95)
HC: 1582183155 ($34.95)

King Philip's War,
by George E. Ellis and John Morris
As Published in 1906.
TP: 1582184305 ($17.95)
HC: 1582184313 ($29.95)

Round the Hub,
by Samuel A. Drake
As Published in 1882.
TP: 1582185182 ($14.95)
HC: 1582185190 ($27.95)

Border Wars of New England,
by Samuel A. Drake
As Published in 1897.
TP: 1582183325 ($15.95)
HC: 1582183333 ($29.95)

The Making of New England,
by Samuel A. Drake
As Published in 1899.
TP: 1582183988 ($14.95)
HC: 1582183996 ($27.95)

The Puritan Age and Rule in Massachusetts 1629-1686,
by George E. Ellis
As Published in 1888.
TP: 1582186200 ($27.95)
HC: 1582186219 ($39.95)

Battle of Bunker Hill,
by George E. Ellis
As Published in 1895.
TP: 158218402X ($9.95)
HC: 1582184038 ($19.95)

Bunker Hill,
by Samuel A. Drake
As Published in 1875.
TP: 1582183295 ($6.95)
HC: 1582183309 ($19.95)

On Plymouth Rock,
by Samuel A. Drake
As Published in 1897.
TP: 1582184348 ($9.95)
HC: 1582184356 ($24.95)

New England Legends and Folk Lore,
by Samuel A. Drake
As Published in 1901.
TP: 1582184429 ($24.95)
HC: 1582184437 ($39.95)

Watch Fires of '76,
by Samuel A. Drake
As Published in 1895.
TP: 1582184704 ($14.95)
HC: 1582184712 ($29.95)

To order any of the above titles:

* Contact your local bookstore and order through *Ingram Books*.
* Contact the publisher directly
  (for general information or special event purchases):

Digital Scanning, Inc.
344 Gannett Rd., Scituate, MA 02066
Phone: (781) 545-2100 Fax: (781) 545-4908 Toll Free in the U.S.: 888-349-4443
email: books@digitalscanning.com
www.digitalscanning.com